MARY
HOPE OF THE WORLD

MARY

HOPE OF THE WORLD

By

Very Rev. James Alberione, S.S.P., S.T.D.

Translation by

Hilda Calabro, M.A.

ST. PAUL EDITIONS

IMPRIMATUR:

✛ RICHARD CARDINAL CUSHING

Library of Congress Catalog Card Number: 59-28503

ISBN 0-8198-0089-9 cloth
      0-8198-0090-2 paper

Printed in the U.S.A., by the Daughters of St. Paul
50 St. Paul's Ave., Boston, MA 02130

The Daughters of St. Paul are an international congregation of religious women serving the Church with the communications media.

ACKNOWLEDGMENTS

Quotations from the New Testament are taken from the Confraternity of Christian Doctrine edition. Quotations from the Old Testament are from the Douay Version.

CONTENTS

INTRODUCTION

I am presenting some brief reflections on the life of Mary Most Holy.

Let us draw near to Mary the better to know her: "To think therefore upon her, is perfect understanding: and he that watcheth for her, shall quickly be secure" (Wis. 6: 16).

Mary anticipates those who seek her and answers them before they call her. Who loves her, seeks her; who seeks her, easily finds her. St. Anselm asserts that desired help is sometimes more readily obtained by invoking Mary's name than by invoking the Name of Jesus, because as Lord and Judge of all, Jesus discerns and weighs everyone's merits, but Mary, being a merciful Mother and not a judge, helps everyone.

The Blessed Virgin's life can be considered under a threefold aspect:

1. **Mary in the divine mind:** She existed in God's thought, in prophecies, and in the longing of humanity.

2. **Mary in her earthly life:** She passed through this life without a shadow of guilt. Destined by God to crush Satan's head, she did not know sin; destined

to be man's co-redemptrix, she corresponded fully to her calling.

3. **Mary in the life of glory:** She lives in Heaven, she lives in the Church, and she lives in the hearts of the faithful, who are continuously blessed by her favors.

PART I

MARY IN THE MIND OF GOD

CHAPTER I

MARY IS FORETOLD

1. Mary was in the mind of God from all eternity.—"I was set up from eternity, and of old before the earth was made" (Prov. 8: 23).

When the Lord ordained the creation of the world, He prepared a scale of beings of varying beauty. It was formed of inanimate and animate creatures—plants, animals and man. Above them God placed the Angels, creatures superior to man because they are pure spirits.

But the most beautiful creature of all, the one in whom all the marvels of the natural and supernatural order are gathered, is Mary. She is God's masterpiece.

The Son, uncreated Wisdom, thought of her from all eternity, and prepared for Himself, in her heart, a worthy tabernacle in which to dwell.

The Holy Spirit, Who was to unite Mary to Himself as His celestial Spouse, willed her to be so rich in sanctity as to surpass all the Angels and Saints from the very moment of her conception: "The foundations thereof are in the holy mountains. Glorious things are said of thee, O city of God" (Ps. 86: 1, 3).

— 19 —

And in Proverbs we read: "The Lord possessed
me in the beginning of His ways, before He made
anything from the beginning. I was set up from
eternity, and of old before the earth was made. The
depths were not as yet, and I was already conceived, neither had the fountains of waters as yet
sprung out: The mountains with their huge bulk
had not as yet been established: before the hills I
was brought forth. He had not yet made the earth,
nor the rivers, nor the poles of the world. When He
prepared the heavens, I was present: when with a
certain law and compass He enclosed the depths:
when He established the sky above, and poised the
fountains of waters: when He compassed the sea
with its bounds, and set a law to the waters that
they should not pass their limits: when He balanced
the foundations of the earth; I was with Him forming all things: and was delighted every day, playing
before Him at all times; playing in the world: and
my delights were to be with the children of men"
(Prov. 8: 22-31).

"From the beginning, and before the world,
was I created, and unto the world to come I shall
not cease to be, and in the holy dwelling place I
have ministered before Him. And so was I established in Sion, and in the holy city likewise I rested,
and my power was in Jerusalem. And I took root
in an honourable people, and in the portion of my
God His inheritance, and my abode is in the full
assembly of saints" (Ecclus. 24: 14-16).

2. **The mind of God in Sacred Scripture.**—The first prophecy was made by God Himself: "I will put enmities between thee and the woman, and thy seed and her seed: she shall crush thy head, and thou shalt lie in wait for her heel" (Gen. 3: 15).

"Behold a Virgin shall conceive, and bear a Son, and His name shall be called Emmanuel" (Isa. 7: 14).

Mary is the rod of Jesse: "And there shall come forth a rod out of the root of Jesse, and a flower shall rise up out of his root" (Isa. 11: 1). The rod of Jesse blossomed: the Virgin bore the God-Man, and the Lord restored peace, reconciling Heaven and earth.

"I was exalted like a cedar in Lebanon, and as a cypress tree on Mount Sion. I was exalted like a palm tree in Cades, and as a rose plant in Jericho. As a fair olive tree in the plains, and as a plane tree by the water in the streets, was I exalted. I gave a sweet smell like cinnamon, and aromatical balm: I yielded a sweet odour like the best myrrh" (Ecclus. 24: 17-20).

"As the vine I have brought forth a pleasant odour: and my flowers are the fruit of honour and riches. I am the mother of fair love, and of fear, and of knowledge, and of holy hope. In me is all grace of the way and of the truth, in me is all hope of life and of virtue" (Ecclus. 24: 23-25).

"Behold my beloved speaketh to me: Arise, make haste, my love, my dove, my beautiful one, and come. For winter is now past, the rain is over and gone. The flowers have appeared in our land, the time of the pruning is come: the voice of the turtle is heard in our land" (Cant. 2: 10-12).

God contemplates Mary, who has formed His delight from all eternity; let us, therefore, as well-beloved children, imitate our Divine Father. He is so pleased with Mary; may we, too, delight to contemplate her greatness.

When we look at Mary, temptations are put to flight, the mind is enlightened, and the passions are calmed. With Mary's help, we triumph over every concupiscence, because nothing can resist her. This is why St. Bernard writes: "In dangers, in sorrows and in doubts, think of Mary, invoke Mary; may her name never cease to be on our lips, may she never depart from our hearts."

Mary always listens to the petitions of those who beg her protection.

All the prophets desired Mary; let us, too, desire her and pray to her. Who finds Mary, finds God and eternal life. "Blessed is the man that heareth me, and that watcheth daily at my gates, and waiteth at the posts of my doors. He that shall find me, shall find life, and shall have salvation from the Lord" (Prov. 8: 34-35).

"Each time I sigh and breathe, I long for you, O Jesus and Mary," a Saint used to say. Who seeks Mary and invokes her, quickly finds her and abundantly draws from her, as from a sea, all sorts of favors and graces.

In every necessity, let us confidently have recourse to this Mother of Mercy; she will always grant our requests.

A Thought from St. Bernard: The Immaculate Virgin was chosen from all eternity; from the very beginning the Most High saw her and prepared her for Himself alone. She was prefigured by the Patriarchs, and announced by the Prophets.

St. Alphonsus de Liguori

The great Marian Doctor of the Church, the singer of Mary's divine glories, is the fervent apostle of a tender and trusting devotion to her.

Alphonsus was born of noble and pious parents near Naples, on September 27, 1606. A few days later he was baptized at the Church of Mary Most Holy of the Virgins, and was placed under her special protection.

His was the singular grace of being brought up by a saintly mother, who instilled in him a tender piety and a great love for Mary Most Holy. Every day Alphonsus prayed to Mary in a transport of delight; he called her his Mother, his Protectress and his Hope. This most charming flower of Mary's garden did not delay long in showing its fruits. He grew in age and in sanctity, and in the midst of grave perils, preserved his baptismal innocence intact.

Deeming himself unworthy of the high dignity of the priesthood, Alphonsus undertook a career in law, and in a short time became one of the most outstanding lawyers. This was not his vocation, however; Mary wanted him a Priest, an apostle.

When he inadvertently compromised a lawsuit, he was so deeply moved that he decided to abandon Law.

Hearing the Lord's call to join His followers, he answered promptly. He overcame the obstacles that were placed in his path by his relatives, and devoted himself to sacred studies with great love. In preparation for the priesthood, he resolved to fast every Saturday in honor of Mary Most Holy, and Mary formed him into a perfect Priest and apostle.

His priestly life was the life of a true apostle, of a sincere lover of Jesus and Mary. His favorite topic for sermons was the Blessed Mother, and with these, he obtained the most striking conversions.

One day, while he was preaching the novena of the Assumption on the coasts of Amalfi, he said, "Behold I am going to pray to Mary for you all, but you ask graces for me, too, at this moment." There was fire in those words. He became radiant, then was lifted upwards over the pulpit toward a picture of the Blessed Virgin. And from this picture, a shaft of light enveloped him.

He was made Bishop of St. Agatha dei Goti, and the good he worked was immense. He wrote one hundred and twenty moral and spiritual works, which are permeated with the sublimest Marian sentiment. In "The Glories of Mary" he compiled the most solid doctrine of the Fathers and Doctors on Mary's privileges, goodness and protection.

Alphonsus died on July 31, 1787, at the ringing of the *Angelus,* assisted by the Blessed Virgin.

O Blessed Virgin, Mother of God, from the depths of my heart I praise and extol you as the purest, the fairest, the holiest creature of all God's handiwork.

CHAPTER II

TYPES OF MARY

There are many types in the Old Testament which, although referring in their true and literal sense to other physical and moral persons, are applied by the Fathers and by the Church in her liturgy to Mary Most Holy.

Many biblical personages make us think of Mary. Israel's heroines cannot be compared to her in sanctity, but as liberators of their people they resemble the Woman who is the conqueror of the serpent and co-redemptrix of the world. God willed that Mary be preceded by a legion of chosen souls, admirable for their virtue, who in some way should foreshadow the **blessed among all women** and set forth for our admiration the characteristics of the Mother of the Savior. Such were Sara, Rachel, Mary, the sister of Moses, Debbora, Jahel, Judith—who, in triumphing over Holofernes, became "the glory of Jerusalem, the joy of Israel and the honor of her people"—and Esther, whose beauty won the King's heart and made all her people find favor in his sight.

Sara was Abraham's wife, but she had no children. Wishing to reward her virtue, God said to

Abraham, "Sarai thy wife thou shalt not call Sarai, but Sara. And I will bless her, and of her I will give thee a son, whom I will bless, and he shall become nations, and kings of people shall spring from him" (Gen. 17: 15-16). Abraham and Sara doubted this promise because they were already old, but the Lord assured them, saying, "Is there anything hard to God? According to appointment I will return to thee at this same time, life accompanying, and Sara shall have a son" (Gen. 18: 14). And so it was. Sara conceived and bore a son.

Mary became a Mother, remaining a Virgin, in a superhuman way; and as Sara gave birth to Isaac, head of the Chosen People, so Mary gave birth to the Redeemer, Founder of the society of the children of God—the Church.

Rachel, daughter of Laban, possessed such a rare beauty that, to have her as his wife, Jacob did not disdain to serve her father almost as his slave for fourteen years. Jacob had two famous sons by Rachel: Joseph and Benjamin. This woman's extraordinary beauty was an eloquent image of Mary's ineffable beauty—beauty which was the fruit of her great virtues. For this reason the Church sings of Mary, "You are all beautiful, O Mary, and in you there is no stain of original sin."

Just as Jacob was attracted by Rachel's beauty, so the Son of God was enraptured by the beauty of the Blessed Virgin. The Archangel Gabriel greeted

her: "Hail, full of grace, the Lord is with thee. Blessed art thou among women" (Luke 1: 28).

Another famous type of the Blessed Virgin was
the gentle sister of Moses, called **Mary**. She succeeded in saving her brother from the cruel death
to which, by order of the King, all Hebrew male
children were to be subjected. She possessed the
gift of prophecy; and she was the leader of the
Hebrew women in the passage through the Red Sea.
It was she who first intoned the hymn of thanksgiving, saying: "Let us sing to the Lord, for He is
gloriously magnified, the horse and his rider He
hath thrown into the sea" (Ex. 15: 21).

Mary Most Holy, too, was endowed with the
gift of prophecy, and immaculately pure, she was
the joyful leader of all virgins. As Satan's conqueror,
she intoned the canticle of a new liberation and redemption, worked by the Word Incarnate in her
most pure womb.

Other noble types of Mary Most Holy were the
great women, **Debbora** and Jahel, who took part in
the defeat and death of Sisara, and consequently in
the salvation of the people of Israel, of whom Sisara was an enemy. Enlightened by the spirit of the
Lord, Debbora ruled the Israelites and judged their
lawsuits. She induced Barac, governor of the people,
to declare war on Sisara's army, and she foretold the
victory by saying that Sisara would die at the hand

of a woman. This woman was Jahel, who gave hospitality to the fleeing Sisara and then nailed his head to the ground. For this reason, Debbora is called the Mother of Israel, and Jahel is hailed as the blessed among women. They are types of Mary Most Holy, Satan's conqueror, she who crushed his head with her foot and gave to the world the Savior, she who was hailed as the blessed among women, the honor and the glory of the Christian people.

Debbora sang her glorious canticle and the Blessed Virgin sang an immortal canticle which was, is, and always will be on the lips of the faithful: "My soul magnifies the Lord" (Luke 1: 46).

Another beautiful type of Mary Most Holy is **Judith.** A powerful monarch of Assyria, wishing to subject all the world to his rule, ordered the terrible Holofernes to march with his army against those nations rebellious to his dominion and force them into submission. Vexed by the resistance of the Hebrews, Holofernes beseiged the city of Bethulia. Provisions were soon lacking, and water, too, for the enemy had taken possession of the springs. Before long, the cry went up that it would be better to surrender than to die.

But a woman inspired by God exclaimed: "And who are you that tempt the Lord? This is not a word that may draw down mercy, but rather that may stir up wrath, and enkindle indignation.... Let us humble our souls before Him. . . . Let us humbly wait for His consolation, and the Lord our God will require our blood of the afflictions of our enemies, and He will humble all the nations that shall rise up against us, and bring them to disgrace" (Judith 8: 11-20). This woman was Judith, a very devout widow in whom the people gloried because, to great beauty, she joined a rare goodness of soul. Inspired from on high, she went to the enemy camp, and when she was delightedly welcomed to the tent of Holofernes, she cut off the proud man's head. While the enemy army fled, the Chosen People unanimously blessed the woman who had delivered them, singing, "Thou art the glory of Jerusalem, thou art the joy of Israel, thou art the honour of our people" (Judith 15: 10).

Judith's beauty is a type of Mary's beauty: in fact, no creature pleased God for splendor of virtue as did Mary who, by becoming the blessed Mother of the Word Incarnate, crushed the head of Satan, the ferocious enemy of mankind, and freed humanity from slavery. For this reason, the Church rightly attributes to Mary the words of the Hebrew people to Judith: "Thou art the glory of Jerusalem, thou art the joy of Israel, thou art the honour of our people."

Esther, a woman of incomparable beauty, won the favor of the King, who had deposed Queen Vasthi from the throne because she provoked him over a trivial matter. In her place he seated the humble Esther. And it was this new queen who saved the Chosen People from the cruel degree of total extermination. Aman, the astute, proud and cruel prime minister, had decreed that all the King's subjects should kneel before him in adoration. Only Mardochai, adorer of the one true God, refused to adore Aman. Indignant, Aman rushed to the King and obtained from him the death sentence for Mardochai and all his countrymen.

Full of faith in God, Esther then presented herself, unsummoned, to the King, to plead on behalf of her people. She did so at the risk of her life, but her charm and her overwhelming beauty saved her and the Hebrew people, too.

Esther is a type of the Blessed Virgin Mary, who won God's love with the splendor of her virtues, drew Him into her heart, and gave to the world the Divine Redeemer.

Let us also try to possess in some manner the sublime virtues of the great Mother of God, and be, in so far as it is possible, living images of Mary.

At the judgment, before admitting us to the splendors of eternal glory, God will examine us to see whether we conform to His Son's image: "Conformed to the image of His Son" (Rom. 8: 29). But whoever is similar to Mary also will be similar to Jesus, the most beautiful of the sons of men, Who resembled His Mother in every way.

*Esther, queen and sovereign, prefigures Mary,
the great Queen, the great Sovereign.*

Whoever imitates Mary gradually will become an image of Jesus, and will be certain of his eternal salvation.

A Thought from St. Bonaventure: The Virgin Mary was admirably symbolized by Judith, of whom it was written: "And she was greatly renowned among all, because she feared the Lord very much, neither was there anyone that spoke an ill word of her" (Judith 8: 8). Mary is renowned among all peoples for her virtues and her holy examples. She is even more famous for her marvels of mercy and unutterably tender care. She is incomparably and supremely illustrious by reason of the graces and the wondrous privileges bestowed upon her by the Lord. What can be more stupendous than being both a Virgin and the Mother of God?

Esther

St. Bonaventure compares Esther to Mary: "Esther presented herself to her most powerful husband, accompanied by two handmaids. She leaned familiarly on one, while the other, walking behind her, held the train of her royal garment. Esther, queen and sovereign, stands for Mary, the great Queen, the great Sovereign. The two companions are the angelic creature and the human creature, for Mary is the true Sovereign of Angels and men.

"King Assuerus represents the Lord, Who grants Mary grace for mankind, extending the sceptre of His omnipotence over her, i.e., giving her for her Son His only Son, Jesus Christ, through Whom and in Whom He reigns in Heaven and upon the earth. Jesus is the Omnipotent Father's royal sceptre. God communicates His omnipotence to Mary. Thus, O Blessed Virgin, you are omnipotent with Him and because of Him.

"All who escape eternal damnation do so through Mary's powerful intercession. Esther's story proves it: the King loved her more than all the other women and he placed the royal diadem on her head. The favor Esther found with Assuerus brought two beneficial results: the royal dignity for herself and salvation for her people from the death to which they had been condemned by the perfidious Aman. Is this not what our Esther, the Most Blessed Virgin Mary, obtained from the Eternal King? She found such great favor with Him that she became Queen and Lady, and saved mankind from the death to which it was condemned. Thus St. Anselm used to say in enthusiastic gratitude: 'What can I ever do for the Mother of my Lord and my God? A prisoner, I was redeemed by the fruit of her womb; condemned to eternal death, I was delivered by her Child. I was lost and her adorable Son rescued me from the exile of my misery; He mercifully led me back to the homeland of eternal happiness.'

"You are the omnipotent Queen who defeated the treacherous Aman, the impure and cruel serpent, the enemy of the human race. You stripped him of his empire, you trampled upon him with your feet, you crushed his head; and he, the deceiving and impious accuser, is condemned to hell. Through you we return to the grace of God. O Sovereign Spouse of the Sovereign King, guard as the apples of your eye the faithful servants of your Jesus; be the consolation of the world and the refuge of your people."

Through you we hope for the remission of our sins, and in you, O blessed Lady, is our hope of reward.

CHAPTER III

OTHER TYPES OF MARY

St. Paul writes that the Old Testament was a type of the New Testament: "Now all these things happened to them as a type" (1 Cor. 10: 11). The Fathers of the Church, authoritative interpreters of Sacred Scriptures, saw this affirmation of the Apostle confirmed in a continuous series of facts, instructions, symbols and rites which fill the history and life of God's Chosen People.

More than all other creatures, Mary Most Holy deserves, by reason of her eminent sanctity and extraordinary prerogatives, all the praises which Sacred Scriptures refer either to the people of Israel or to the Church.

The Mother of God and of mankind symbolizes and sums up in herself the entire faithful side of humanity. Consequently, the types relating to the Church refer to Mary, just as all that is said of the kingdom eminently refers to the queen.

All that is written of Jerusalem, the spiritual homeland of every believer, can be repeated of Mary: "Glorious things are said of thee, O City of God" (Ps. 86: 3).

Mary is the shining rainbow which appeared in the heavens to remind the Most High of His mer-

ciful alliance with men. She is the **Eden** of delights,
Noe's Ark, the mysterious **ladder of Jacob,** whose
steps joined earth to Heaven. She is the **burning
bush** in which God manifested Himself to Moses.
She is the **rod of Aaron.** She is **Gedeon's fleece,
Solomon's Temple,** the **Ark of the Covenant.** Mary
is the **little cloud** that the Prophet Elias, from the
summit of Mount Carmel, saw rising up from the
sea after long years of drought.

Mary was foreshadowed by the **land of Eden,**
the land of grace, in which, before the sin, "the
Lord God had planted a paradise of pleasure from
the beginning; wherein He placed man whom He
had formed. And the Lord God brought forth of
the ground all manner of trees, fair to behold, and
pleasant to eat of: the tree of life also in the midst
of paradise: and the tree of knowledge of good and
evil. And a river went out of the place of pleasure
to water paradise, which from thence is divided into four heads" (Gen. 2: 8-10). This Eden of such
great beauty is a type of Mary. God is the One Who
waters it, and the water He uses is grace, with
which Mary is flooded. St. John Damascene writes:
"Mary is the spiritual Eden, holier and more divine
than the ancient Eden, for in that one Adam dwelt,
whereas in Mary God made His abode."

Other types of Mary are **Noe's Ark** and the **Ark
of the Covenant.** The **Ark** saved Noe and his family
from the deluge; Mary saved the human race

through Jesus Christ. Noe's Ark floated on the same waters in which the world was drowning; Mary was untouched by the slimy waters of concupiscence and sin. Those who took refuge in Noe's Ark were rescued from death; those who take refuge in Mary do not drown in the flood of passions. The earth was repopulated by those who had taken refuge in the Ark; Heaven is inhabited by Mary's faithful servants.

St. Ambrose expresses the points of similarity between the **Ark of the Covenant** and the Blessed Virgin in the following terms: "The Ark contained the tables of the Law; Mary gave shelter in her womb to the Heir of the Testament. The Ark bore the Law; Mary bore the Gospel. In the Ark the voice of God made itself heard; Mary gave us the very Word of God. The Ark shone with the purest gold; both internally and externally Mary shone with the splendor of virginity. But the gold which adorned the Ark was taken from the depths of the earth, while the gold with which Mary shone was taken from the mines of Heaven." Thus the Church justifiably invokes Mary under the title of **Ark of the Covenant.**

Jacob's ladder is also a type of Mary. After receiving his father Isaac's blessing, Jacob headed for Mesopotamia. When he had gone a short distance, he stopped to rest and fell asleep. "And he saw in his sleep a ladder standing upon the earth, and the top thereof touching Heaven: the Angels also of God ascending and descending by it. And the Lord leaning upon the ladder, saying to him: I am the Lord God of Abraham thy father, and the God of Isaac; the land, wherein thou sleepest, I will give to thee and to thy seed. And thy seed shall be as the dust of the earth: thou shalt spread abroad to the west, and to the east, and to the north, and to the south: and in thee and thy seed all the tribes of the earth shall be blessed. And I will be thy keeper whithersoever thou goest, and will bring thee back into this land: neither will I leave thee, till I have accomplished all that I have said" (Gen. 28: 12-15).

Mary is the ladder that God made for Himself, and by means of which He descended from Heaven to earth, assuming mortal flesh in her. And, having become true man, He forever reunited the creature to the Creator.

The **rod of Aaron**, too, was a type of Mary. The Lord said to Moses· "Speak to the children of Israel, and take of every one of them a rod by their kindreds, of all the princes of the tribes, twelve rods, and write the name of every man upon his rod. And the name of Aaron shall be for the tribe of Levi, and one rod shall contain all their families. And thou shalt lay them up in the tabernacle of the covenant before the testimony, where I will speak to thee. Whomsoever of these I shall choose, his rod shall blossom" (Num. 17: 2-5). This rod which blossomed miraculously without root or nourishment was a type of Mary who, having become the living temple of the Holy Spirit, conceived without human intervention that blessed fruit which gives spiritual life to all: Jesus Christ.

Gedeon's fleece presents us with another type of Mary, and the dew, which wets it in the silence of the night, represents the descent of the Word into the Virgin's most pure womb. "It is most proper," exclaims St. Ambrose, "to compare Mary to Gedeon's fleece, because she conceived the Lord and was entirely imbued with Him as with sweet dew, without any damage to her virginity."

Mary was also prefigured by the glorious **Temple of Solomon.** This great King destined the Temple for God's habitation; he had it built with extraordinary magnificence, lavished gold and silver upon it and adorned it with rare wood and precious stones. Within it he enclosed the Ark of the Covenant, which contained the tables of the Law. The Temple was decorated with all that wealth and the best art together could produce. Such magnificence signified the stupendous dowry of Mary's virtues. She is the temple enclosing the Holy of Holies within herself; she is the temple of the Lord.

There are many other types of Mary in Sacred Scripture: Mary is the cedar of Lebanon, the palm of Cades, the rose of Jericho, the sealed fountain, the garden enclosed, etc.

The Church has always delighted in these types and has applied them in her liturgy to Mary.

Let us, too, study such types and recall them with delight, associating with them the blessed name of Mary Most Holy.

A Thought from St. Bonaventure: O Virgin of Virgins! You have mounted to Him Who sits on the heavenly throne, to the Lord's majesty, and this does not surprise us, for the roots of your humility ascend to the heights of Heaven. Down this ladder the Angel of the great Council descended to you when He came to take upon Himself the infirmities of our nature, and up this very ladder the Angels of the earth, that is, those who live as Angels upon the earth, ascend to Heaven.

Let us try to rise through Mary to Him Who through Mary descended to us. Through her we shall find favor with Jesus Who through Mary burdened Himself with our miseries.

A List of Marian Symbols

Mary is compared to:
The wine, the oil poured out, the odor of ointments (Cant. 1: 1-3);
The tents of Cedar, the curtains of Solomon (Cant. 1: 4);
The sun, the vineyard (Cant. 1: 5);
The bundle of myrrh (Cant. 1: 12);

The flower of the field, the lily of the valleys (Cant. 2: 1);

The dove in the clefts of the rock (Cant. 2: 14);

The pillar of smoke of aromatical spices, of myrrh ... (Cant. 3: 6);

The doves' eyes (Cant. 4: 1);

The tower of David (Cant. 4: 4);

The dropping honeycomb (Cant. 4: 11);

The pillars of marble (Cant. 5: 15);

The army set in array (Cant. 6: 3);

The morning rising, the moon, the sun (Cant. 6: 9);

The mouth of the Most High (Ecclus. 24: 5);

The light that never fails (Ecclus. 24: 6);

The pillar of a cloud (Ecclus. 24: 7);

The circuit of Heaven, the bottom of the deep (Ecclus. 24: 8);

The cypress tree on Mount Sion (Ecclus. 24: 17);

The fair olive tree in the plains, the plane tree by the water in the streets (Ecclus. 24: 19);

The cinnamon and aromatical balm (Ecclus. 24: 20);

The best myrrh (Ecclus. 24: 20).

O Mother of tender mercy, you are our light in uncertainty, our comfort in sorrow, our solace in the time of trial, our refuge from every peril and temptation.

PART II

MARY'S LIFE ON EARTH

CHAPTER I

THE BIRTH OF MARY

After having considered Mary in the mind of God, in the vision of the Prophets, and in Old Testament types, let us consider her life on earth from her Immaculate Conception until her glorious Assumption into Heaven.

The Prophets had given the Chosen People an infallible criterion for recognizing the advent of the Savior. A **sign** was to appear: a virgin, remaining a virgin, would become the Mother of the Messias—the Desired of nations. The Hebrew people were watching the root of Jesse, the royal line of David, out of which the **great sign** was to rise: **Behold a virgin shall conceive.**

The hour of redemption was about to strike; all awaited the sign of Isaias: "And there shall come forth a rod out of the root of Jesse, and a flower shall rise up out of his root" (Isa. 11: 1).

The beautiful figure of Mary appeared as a sun: "As the sun when it riseth to the world" (Ecclus. 26: 21). And this radiant sun had its dawning in Mary's Immaculate Conception, in her birth and in the bestowing of her name.

1. **The Immaculate Conception.**—Mary appeared full of grace, all beautiful, all holy. "She,"

writes St. Ambrose, "is the rod on which there was never the knot of original sin nor the bark of actual sin." St. Ephrem calls Mary, "the Spouse of God, who reconciled us to Him." St. Germanus of Constantinople calls her, "the most admirable of everything admirable." St. John Damascene says: "She is a profound abyss of miracles, a boundless ocean of gifts, the innocent one par excellence, the Immaculate one, the undefiled one, the incorrupt one, the all-modest Virgin, the Mother of God and our Lady."

Some Fathers of the Church, enraptured by Mary's beauty, called her: "Purest dove, holy Jerusalem, superb throne of God, ark of sanctification built by the Eternal Wisdom, Queen full of delights leaning upon her Beloved, born of the Heart of God, dear to Him, all beautiful, free from the shadow of sin, lily among thorns, virgin soil, spotless Virgin, immaculate Virgin, always blessed!"

How is it possible, however, to contemplate a beautiful fruit without thinking of the plant that produced it? St. Joachim and St. Anne were Mary's fortunate parents. Their names were given to us by tradition.

They were endowed with faith, hope and charity, filled with every virtue. Through their prayer and fasting they hastened the redemption of Israel. Thus Joachim, the chosen soul whose name means preparation of the Lord, and his wife Anne, whose name means grace, gave birth to the Lady, to the Queen of Heaven and earth.

Mary is the bright glory of St. Joachim and St. Anne. Good children are truly the honor and glory of their parents.

What great fortune for the Church and the state to have good families! Oh, if only all families were well ordered and founded upon the Sacrament of Matrimony!

Vocations to the religious and ecclesiastical life are often born in good families. Our first duty, therefore, is to pray for the sanctification of families; secondly, we must be grateful to God for having disposed that we should be born into good families. Let us ask the Lord to raise up holy vocations among our relatives.

2. **Mary's birth.**—Mary was conceived the most beautiful creature, not only exempt from sin, but clothed with so much grace that she surpassed the very Angels themselves and the Saints. In the liturgy of Mary's Nativity, the Church sings, "The birth of the glorious Virgin Mary brought joy to the entire world."

St. John Damascene says, "I greet you, lamb, in whom the good Shepherd will soon come to take on human flesh, which will permit Him to be the Lamb of God, the true paschal Lamb immolated for the redemption of His people."

Mary's birthplace is unknown. Some think that it was Sephoris, others Bethlehem, and still others Nazareth.

Western tradition holds that Mary's native city was Nazareth. In the office of the Holy House we read, in fact, that the Holy House of Loreto, which came from Nazareth, received the first cries of the infant Mary.

Mary's birth filled Heaven and earth with joy. God the Father rejoiced, as He lovingly contemplated in that tiny infant, His immaculate daughter and the Mother of the Eternal Word. God the Son rejoiced as He contemplated in her His most beloved Mother. God the Holy Spirit rejoiced as He took delight in His masterpiece and contemplated in her His most pure and faithful Spouse. The Angels rejoiced as they hailed her their royal sovereign. Finally, humanity rejoiced, for in her it recognized the long-awaited dawn of that divine Sun—the Redeemer, Who was to drive away the darkness of sin.

Let us exultantly hail Mary the celestial child, the temple of purest gold into which Jesus will enter when the fullness of time comes.

Let us thank the Lord for having given us such a great and good Mother.

Oh, the beauty of Mary's soul! "All the glory of the King's daughter is within" (Ps. 44: 14). External beauty does not count with God; virtue and grace do.

3. **The name of Mary.**—Fifteen days after their child's birth, Joachim and Anne gave her the name of Mary. This most holy, most sweet, and most worthy name suits the Virgin perfectly. It came from the treasures of the Divinity and was given to her to express the dignity of the role to which the Lord had preordained her.

Mary's name signifies: a) Star of the sea, b) Enlightener, and c) Lady.

Mary is the star of the sea, because she shows poor mortals, who are tossed about by passions, the shortest and safest way to reach the longed-for haven. **Hail, star of the sea;** you are the brightly shining star from which proceeds the brilliant ray of the God-Man. You are a most helpful star, lighting up our way by the examples of your life, by the blessings of your mercy, by the splendor of your glory.

The name Mary also means Lady: the Lady par excellence, the Lady of Heaven and earth. She is the star of the sea for men, enlightener of Angels, Lady of the universe.

Therefore, the name Mary was not given to the Virgin of Nazareth by chance; it was significant of the seeds of virtues, reposing in the child, which would develop to the point of most sublime perfection.

"Mary's name," writes one of the Fathers of the Church, "refreshes the weary, cures the weak, enlightens the blind, touches the hardened, comforts the struggling, and shakes off Satan's yoke. Upon hearing it, Heaven rejoices, the earth exults, the Angels are gladdened, the demons tremble, and hell is disturbed." Like the Name of Jesus, Mary's name is "honey to the mouth, harmony to the ear, and joy to the heart."

Let us honor, invoke and defend Mary's name. Let us honor the name of the Virgin who is the Immaculate, the One full of grace, the Queen of the universe. Let us invoke this name in dangers, in temptations, in sorrows and in tribulations. Let us defend the name of Mary by blessing it when the wicked profane it.

A Thought from St. Peter Damian:—Let us rejoice in the consideration of the Blessed Virgin's nativity; yes, let us rejoice at this birth as we do for the birth of Christ Himself. Today the Queen of the world is born to us, the Gate of Heaven, the Tabernacle of the Lord, the Ladder of Heaven by which the King of eternity will descend to our lowliness, and by means of which man the sinner will be able to ascend again to his God.

Councils in Favor of the Immaculate Conception

The Council of Ephesus: It was the third ecumenical council (431); it called Mary Immaculate, that is, without stain of sin.

The Council of Toledo: This council was held in 634. It approved and praised the missal reformed by St. Isidore, Archbishop of Seville. In it the Office of the Conception was marked for the entire Octave. Moreover, it declared that the Virgin was preserved from original sin by a privilege rightly due to the dignity of the Mother of God.

The Eleventh Council of Toledo of 675: It confirmed the doctrine of St. Ildephonsus and, with him, confessed that Mary was never stained by original sin.

The Third Council of Constantinople: This was held in 680, under the Pontificate of St. Agatho. A letter written by Sophronius, the Patriarch of Jerusalem, was received with unusual applause. In this letter Mary was called, "Immaculate, that is, holy in body and soul and free from every sin or stain of sin."

The Second Council of Nicaea: Convened in 787 and ratified by Pope Adrian I, it spoke of the Blessed Virgin, calling her, "Most holy and Immaculate, beyond reproach, purer than all nature—sensible as well as intellectual" that is, purer than the Angels in Heaven who never sinned either by actual or original sin.

The Council of Basilea: It declared itself for Mary's Immaculate Conception.

The Council of Trent: In the fifth session (1546), this council declared that in the decree concerning original sin, the Blessed Virgin Mother of God was not included.

In 1854, *Pope Pius IX* defined the dogma of the Immaculate Conception of the Blessed Virgin Mary.

In 1950, *Pope Pius XII* defined the dogma of the Assumption of the Blessed Virgin Mary.

O dearest and most clement Virgin Mother, you are our hope most sure and sacred in God's sight, to Whom be honor and glory.

CHAPTER II

THE PRESENTATION IN THE TEMPLE

Divine Providence, which guides everything with firmness and sweetness, was watching over the child Mary, and preparing her for the high position of Mother of God. Toward this end, by means of her parents, God led the heavenly child to the Temple of Jerusalem.

1. **The Presentation in the Temple.**—Tradition narrates that in gratitude to the Lord for the blessing of a daughter, Joachim and Anne vowed to consecrate her to Him in the Temple as soon as her age permitted it. And they were faithful to their promise.

Mary was scarcely three years old when, accompanied by her parents, she first set foot in the Temple. Here the noble child was admitted to the elect group of virgins consecrated to God. The exact time of Mary's presentation in the Temple is unknown. The Church celebrates the feast of the Presentation on November twenty-first.

The purpose of Mary's presentation in the Temple was twofold: that she might consecrate herself to the Lord and receive a suitable spiritual formation.

Presentation of the Child Mary   Titian

*Mary ascended the steps of the Temple,
radiant with joyful eagerness.*

In the left nave of St. Peter's Basilica in Rome there is an altar in honor of the Presentation. A splendid mosaic represents the Virgin as she is being presented in the Temple. There Mary can be seen ascending the steps of the Temple, radiant with joyful eagerness. The priest is greeting her warmly.

Who will tell us of Mary's angelic life in the Temple? "Her mind," writes St. Ambrose, "was always absorbed in the Supreme Good. Her humility, her obedience and her modesty, which is a girl's most valuable asset, matched her silence. To use every minute of the day for the honor of God, she combined mental activity with manual labor. Her soul was never tempted to sloth, and necessity alone made her take repose. Even then, she kept watch in the presence of the Supreme Goodness, dreaming of the glories of the Lord and the wisdom of the divine word, which she had read during the day."

Mary lived for prayer, for study and for work. Every day she meditated upon the great truths. She spoke little but wisely, she often conversed with Angels, and the Lord revealed the mysteries of His mercy to her.

What example the child Mary gave, from the shadow of the sanctuary to girls of all times! Oh, if only all girls would walk in her footsteps, if only they would imitate her virtues!

Whoever leaves the world for the silence and recollection of religious life, following Mary's example, has much for which to thank God. This is such a great grace that it merits the deepest gratitude. Let us ask the grace to learn to live like Mary and to follow in the holy footsteps of her childhood.

2. **Vow of virginity.**—In presenting Mary to the Temple, her parents offered her to God; but she also took an active part in the sacrifice of herself to the Lord.

It is a common belief that Mary was the first among all women to consecrate her virginity to God with an unconditional and irrevocable promise. That is to say, she emitted a formal and explicit vow. Proof of this is found in her reply to the Angel: "How shall this happen, since I do not know man?" (Luke 1: 34).

St. Augustine observes that Mary never would have requested such an explanation if she had not already consecrated herself to the Lord.

Hence we can conclude that the Most Blessed Virgin not only proposed to observe perpetual virginity but that she bound herself to it by a vow.

3. **Mary's Life in the Temple.**—St. Jerome writes: "Hardly had the Blessed Virgin entered the Temple when she imposed upon herself an admirable rule of life: from early morning until nine o'clock, she devoted herself to prayer; from nine

until three in the afternoon she attended to external
activities; then she returned to prayer until the Angel appeared to bring her daily bit of nourishment.
She was as always the first at nocturnal vigils, she
studied the Law of the Lord with more diligence
than the others, she surpassed the most humble in
humility; Mary chanted David's songs with greater
grace, she practised the works of charity with more
fervor, she was the purest among the chaste, and
she possessed all virtues in a greater degree. She
was firm and constant, and every day she grew in
grace and sweetness. Her words were all filled with
grace, and when near her, people felt the presence
of God. She was always at prayer and unceasingly
meditated upon the Law of the Lord. She never
ceased to bless God, and when she was greeted,
instead of replying with the ordinary words of
courtesy, she would reply, 'Thanks be to God.' "
St. Anselm says, "This blessed child was most delicate; she loved the sacred truths and had herself
fully instructed in them. She served the priests joyfully. Hers was the habit of speaking little and of
obeying promptly. She was modest, serene, and full
of sweetness. She greeted everyone with kindness,
and her graciousness and beauty made her greatly
admired."

Mary sanctified her days by the exact ob-
servance of her duties. Even in all domestic duties

she distinguished herself for the exactness, the simplicity and the perfection with which she performed them.

Love of God is shown by the constant and diligent fulfillment of one's duties. Mary sanctified herself by doing well all that the Lord asked of her. We, too, shall sanctify ourselves if we imitate her.

A Thought from St. John Damascene: The Virgin rejected the thought of all earthly things and embraced every virtue. She progressed to such a degree of perfection that she soon deserved to be made the worthy temple of God.

St. Ephrem

The life of St. Ephrem is the life of a great ascetic and mystic, as well as of a most active Apologist and adversary of all heresies.

He was born of pagan parents in Mesopotamia in 306, during the reign of Constantine the Great, when Christianity was spreading rapidly everywhere. As soon as Ephrem came to know the Christian Faith, he embraced it enthusiastically. When his father grew aware of his conversion, he turned him out of the house. Bearing love of religion as his only possession, Ephrem then went to the Bishop of his city. Here he revealed the rarity of his talents to such an extent that although he was only twenty-five, he was assigned to a teaching position and ordained a deacon. Later, Ephrem retired to Edessa where he spent the rest of his life. It was there that he wrote the greater part of his works, which have come down to us. He lived as an anchorite on a mountain where it was possible for many disciples to gather about him. Both the hidden and apostolic lives of these men were of utmost importance in that century. There the great champions of the Greek Catholic Church were formed.

St. Ephrem's devotion to the Blessed Virgin Mary was something out of the ordinary, as his numerous writings on the Blessed Virgin attest. These works could only have been the fruit of a sublime mind occupied wholly with the thought of Mary and of the tenderest of hearts which, not content to have tasted the ineffable sweetness of such a love, desired to share it with others.

The fundamental thought of St. Ephrem's Marian doctrine is that Mary's sublime prerogatives, described by him, so amply and richly, are a natural consequence of the privilege reserved to her of being the Mother of Jesus. Having established this principle, Ephrem proceeds to affirm, with a logical chain of reasoning, that Mary Most Holy was conceived without sin. He sets forth the truth with admirable clarity and says, "Mary was immaculate and free of even the least sin."

St. Ephrem's motive in all his writings on the Virgin is to imbue us with a great trust in Mary, and to make us love her with a love similar to the love borne her by the Celestial Father, Whose daughter she is, by Jesus Christ, Whose Mother she is, by the Holy Spirit, Whose mystical Spouse she is.

And let us, who know our great need for Mary, repeat often with St. Ephrem during the course of our trial on earth, "O Immaculate Virgin, protect us and guard us beneath the wings of your tender pity."

Immaculate Virgin, who directed every movement of your most pure heart toward God, obtain for me the grace to hate sin with all my heart and to live in perfect resignation to the will of God.

CHAPTER III

MARY'S YOUTH

True devotees of Mary are those who imitate her virtues. Children of Mary are her imitators. By imitating Mary we shall draw close to Jesus: to Jesus through Mary.

1. **Mary in the loss of her parents.**—It is commonly believed that the Blessed Virgin lost her beloved parents when she was about eleven. Just when she was living a life of angelic happiness in the House of the Lord, Mary had to taste of that chalice which fills the hearts of children with the most human sadness.

The precise time of Joachim's and Anne's blessed passing is unknown, but the Fathers affirm that Mary became an orphan when still in the Temple. Where were Mary's parents buried? It is not easy to say. Anselm of Cracow wrote that they were buried at Jerusalem.

At the loss of her parents, Mary showed herself perfectly conformed to the will of God and she undoubtedly exclaimed: "May Thy will be done, O Lord!" Her faith and hope made her see in the death of her beloved parents the passage from exile to homeland, from earth to Heaven, from labor to repose. What a lesson for us who, because of too natural an affection, often cannot resign ourselves to the loss of our loved ones. St. Paul warns us that in such circumstances we must not despair as those who have no faith: "For here we have no permanent city, but we seek for the city that is to come" (Heb. 13: 14).

Separation from our dear ones is temporary: we shall see them again someday in our heavenly Home, because even for us the hour will come for rendering an account.

Another reason for being consoled at such times is love of God. He willed it this way: "The Lord gave, and the Lord hath taken away: as it hath pleased the Lord so is it done: blessed be the name of the Lord" (Job 1: 21).

We must take good care of the dying, and with Christian charity prepare them for the great step. We must see to it that they receive the Sacraments in time, assist them, pray for them, lay them out properly and respectfully, give them decent burial, and pray often for the repose of their souls.

2. **Mary's gifts of body.**—In Mary were all those qualities which were to grace the humanity of Christ, the most beautiful among the sons of men: "Thou art beautiful above the sons of men" (Ps. 44: 3). The Spouse of the Sacred Canticles vividly depicts not only the mystical beauty but

also the natural beauty of her Beloved: "My beloved is white and ruddy, chosen out of thousands" (Cant. 5: 10).

Mary's beauty was similar: it was a beauty that won the love not only of the sons of men but even of the very Son of God, Who calls her all beautiful and immaculate: "Thou art all fair, O my love, and there is not a spot in thee" (Cant. 4: 7). Mary is beautiful and she breathes sweetness and grace. "The sun and moon are dazzled by the Virgin's beauty," writes St. Peter Damian. In Mary, in fact, there is all the nobility of birth, of blood, of body, of spirit, of heart and especially of grace and of virtue. This beauty is so radiant that it inspired God the Father to choose her as His dearest Daughter, God the Son to choose her as His Mother, and God the Holy Spirit to choose her as His Spouse. "O most beautiful beauty of all beauties. O Mother of God, supreme ornament of all beauties!" (George of Nicodemia).

What creature can be found sweeter, more beautiful or more marvellous than Mary? She is a world of beauty who enraptures the Creator; men and Angels who upon first seeing her, exclaimed in ecstasy, "Who is she that cometh forth as the morning rising, fair as the moon, bright as the sun, terrible as an army set in array?" (Cant. 6: 9). St. Bernard says that God placed in Mary all the beauties of the universe. Mary is the dawn that precedes the divine Sun, the ornament of the Church, the splendor of the centuries. Her beauty is reflected in the Saints and the Angels.

But what is this beauty? It is both a natural and supernatural beauty which springs from grace, and which attained to the ideal in Mary. It is beauty which shines on the face, enraptures the senses and goes to the heart.

Grace reflects its beauty upon the body, too. Just as vice is reflected in the body, rendering it revolting at times, so, too, goodness, grace, sanctity, and virtue shed a celestial light on the countenance. There is no doubt, then, that the fire of divine love with which Mary burned was reflected in her whole outward appearance, so that she whose purity was angelic was angelic also in countenance.

There was nothing reprehensible, unbecoming or unseemly in Mary's soul or body. Everything in her was the most beautiful work of Divine Wisdom. O Virgin, worthy of the Lord Who is dignity by essence; beautiful in the presence of infinite Beauty; immaculate in the presence of Him Who knows no corruption; great before the Most High; the Mother of God; the Spouse of the Eternal King.

Let us learn to cultivate true virtue, interior beauty; may our soul never be stained by sin! Let us cultivate and increase grace in us. Let us mortify our body and always respect it as the temple of the Holy Spirit.

The Virgin in the Temple   Murillo

*The Virgin Mary is the model for people
of all ages and of all conditions.*

3. **Mary's girlhood virtues.**—Some writers speaking of the girlhood of Mary, say that she practised extraordinary virtues in an extraordinary way. This is not so. True, extraordinary virtues shone in Mary, but she practised them all in a simple and ordinary manner. She loved prayer, sacred chant and the reading of Sacred Scripture but she was always prompt to leave them when obedience required it. Everything in her was orderly, regulated, holy and dignified: she was perfect in the common and ordinary things. "What can you present me that is more perfect than Mary? Neither Prophets, nor Apostles, nor Martyrs, nor Thrones, nor Dominations, nor Powers, nor any visible or invisible creature. What perfection Mary showed in all the circumstances of her life! How admirable she was in the accomplishment of all her duties! She is the model for people of all ages and of all conditions; she is especially the model of all virgins consecrated to the Lord. Whether we must act or pray or obey or humiliate ourselves, Mary is the example for all of us. What rectitude in her desires! What simplicity in her actions! What courage in tribulations! What great patience in trials! What charity for her neighbors! What fervor in prayer! What love of God! What modesty in her person! What humility in her conduct! Everything is admirable in Mary" (St. John Chrysostom).

Mary attained to the highest degree of sanctity in the exercise of common virtues, in the performance of humble duties, and in the fulfillment of her mission.

Mary is a masterpiece of sanctity. She reflects the virtues of Jesus Christ, but her sanctity is the most simple, free from those clamorous deeds which dazzle and deafen one. It is a sanctity which can be imitated in all states of life under all conditions.

Behold the sublime model which must be for us the object of meditation and of imitation. Let us unceasingly concentrate upon our celestial Mother's perfect life so as to reproduce it in our actions.

Let us model our lives on Mary's.

A Thought from St. Ambrose: Here the mirror of virginity is delineated for you. Mary's life was such that it can serve as an example for all. If we love Mary we must love her actions. Whoever aspires to share her reward must also imitate her examples.

St. Ignatius Martyr

St. Ignatius Martyr is one of the greatest figures, one of the strongest characters of early Christianity. He was fortunate to have been a contemporary of the Blessed Virgin and to have been personally acquainted with her.

During Trajan's persecution St. Ignatius was condemned to martyrdom and sent to Rome in chains.

Mary was the love of St. Ignatius. He defended her virginity and called her the Tabernacle of the Word Incarnate. He declared her the Mother of God. He affirmed that no devotee of Mary will ever perish.

St. Ignatius died as a martyr in Rome in the year 107. He was devoured by wild beasts as he himself had desired. Of his body there remained only a few bones. The Christians gathered them up and brought them to Antioch where they were the object of great veneration.

O heart of Mary, heart most like to the Heart of Jesus, pour into my heart the love of your virtues, so that I may become ever closer to Your divine Son.

CHAPTER IV

MARY'S ESPOUSALS

It was God's will that the Blessed Virgin should be united in matrimony to the chaste St. Joseph. There were many reasons for this. According to St. Thomas, it was fitting that Christ be born of a married Virgin and this for Himself, for His Mother, and for us. It was fitting **for Himself**, so that His geneology might be established according to the husband's name, and that He might have a protector and provider as soon as He was born. **For His Mother** it was fitting so that no one should cast suspicion on her innocence, so that she would not be punished by the law for becoming a mother without being lawfully wed, and so that she would have in St. Joseph an irrefutable witness of her virginal purity. **For us** it was fitting that virgins might be taught to preserve the treasure of their good reputation unblemished.

1. **God watches over souls who act out of love for Him.**—Mary had consecrated herself totally to God and intended to serve Him alone, remaining a virgin. But because she was a virgin, the Lord had chosen her to be the Mother of His Son and had

disposed that she should become the spouse of Joseph. And Mary obeyed.

Among the Hebrews the ceremony of Matrimony consisted of two parts: the **betrothal** with the registration of the names in the public records, and the bride's **departure** from her home to the dwelling of her husband. In the betrothal, the agreements and the conditions of the marriage were established: the husband promised to honor his wife, to provide the necessities of life and especially to be faithful. When the time of waiting was over, the ceremony of the wife's departure took place, and all the relatives were invited to make the occasion more solemn. The lapse of time between Mary's betrothal and her entrance into Joseph's house is unknown. St. John Damascene writes: "Having reached the age when she could no longer live in the Temple, Mary was given to Joseph as his spouse by the priests."

But who was Joseph? Sacred Scripture says that he was a **just man,** words which are equal to the highest praise. Joseph, according to the geneology given by St. Matthew and St. Luke, was a descendant of the family of David. In Joseph's time, however, the family of David no longer sat on the throne, having lost the scepter. Always upright and blameless, Joseph, in his youth, was most exemplary. For this reason he was chosen by God to be the spouse of Mary. Joseph's age at the time of his marriage is unknown; it is certain, however, that he was older than his bride. Christian art usually depicts St. Joseph as past the prime of life, out of respect for the Virgin Mary, and also to indicate the control he had over concupiscence.

What promises and obligations were exchanged between the two spouses? St. Augustine answers: "In the union of Mary with Joseph, there was a contract of mutual donation. And it is here, precisely in their mutual donation, that we must admire the triumph of purity, associated with the reality of this matrimony. Between Mary and Joseph there existed a true marriage by reason of which each gave himself to the other. But in what manner did they give themselves to each other? They gave each other their virginity, and regarding this virginity, they yielded to each other a mutual right. Mary had the right to guard Joseph's virginity, and Joseph had the right to guard Mary's virginity. Neither could dispose of their virginity, and the total fidelity of this matrimony consisted in protecting virginity. This was the promise that joined them; this was the pact that bound them. Two virginities were joined to preserve each other. They remind us of two stars, which do not unite except to combine their light. Such was the bond of this matrimony."

Although bound by a vow so contrary to marriage, Mary accepted her union with Joseph, for she always trusted in Divine Providence and let God guide her in all things. Let us do our duty with simplicity, with the right intention, and let us trustingly abandon ourselves in God.

2. **God united two very holy souls so that they might help one another.**—From the Temple in Jerusalem Mary went to Nazareth with her holy husband. In receiving Mary, Joseph's fortunate home received the sun which lighted up everything. Joseph became aware of this in contemplating this marvellous creature more perfect than the Angels, who had transformed his modest home into the most delightful haven of peace, of affection, and of order.

Mary was beautiful, sweetly beautiful when absorbed in prayer, beautiful when performing her domestic duties, beautiful when, in the most secluded corner of the house, she labored for her little Jesus, her God, Who was to call her **Mama**!

The Lord unites the souls He wishes to sanctify. There was nothing earthly in the union between Mary and Joseph; everything bore a celestial imprint. Their lives were united that they might rise to God with doubled fervor.

Joseph was the guardian whom God chose to protect His Mother's purity; and she, by her presence, and her manner, enkindled in her spouse an even greater love of chastity. Let us look at

The Espousals of the Virgin

Joseph was the guardian
whom God chose to protect His Mother's purity.

Mary and Joseph and let us model our lives on their example.

3. **The mysterious manner in which this matrimony took place.**—The Gospel narrates that Mary was with child by the Holy Spirit before she went to live with St. Joseph. And he, "being a just man, and not wishing to expose her to reproach, was minded to put her away privately" (Matt. 1: 19)

These few words reveal the turmoil in Joseph's soul and the struggle going on within him. On the one hand, he knew Mary's eminent virtues and her angelic purity; on the other hand, the time for the solemn ceremony of introducing his spouse into his home having arrived, he felt that he could not go through with it since the law forbade it. Mary was a virgin, a most pure virgin, and Joseph, more than any one else, knew this well: suspicion would have been blasphemy in his eyes. And yet Mary though a Virgin was also a Mother. How act in the conflict between his persuasion of Mary's innocence and the law which, by forbidding the celebration of the espousals, would expose her to public disgrace? Being a just man, Joseph was minded to separate from Mary, and he sought God's direction as to how he should carry out his plan. "Not being able to speak to men," wrote St. Peter Chrysologus, "he confided everything to God in prayer." So as not to arouse evil suspicions regarding Mary, he resolved to put her away privately. It is easy also to imagine Mary's state of mind in those days. Yet her humility prevented her from revealing the great mystery and the supreme dignity to which God had elevated her. She was certain that God would take care of everything, and she was not mistaken.

An Angel of the Lord appeared to Joseph in a dream and said, "Do not be afraid, Joseph, son of David, to take to thee Mary thy wife, for that which is begotten in her is of the Holy Spirit. And she shall bring forth a Son: and thou shalt call His name Jesus; for He shall save His people from their sins" (Matt. 1: 20-21).

The light had come, the clouds were dispersed. Joseph had been informed of the mysteries of the Incarnation, and his respect for Mary's sanctity took on even greater proportions.

Awakening from his dream, Joseph did as the Angel of the Lord had ordered, and he took to himself Mary his wife.

Let us learn to confide in God, and to have recourse to Him in all our difficulties: "Cry to Me and I shall hear you" (Jer. 33: 3).

A Thought from St. Augustine: Fearlessly place all your trust in God and cast yourselves into His arms because He will never cease to lift you to Himself and will never permit anything to happen to you which is not good for you, although you may not understand why.

Robert Bellarmine

Robert Bellarmine was born in Montepulciano on October 4, 1548, of a noble family, lacking in material goods but rich in faith. His mother, Lady Cynthia Cervini, the sister of Pope Marcellus II, instilled sentiments of deep piety together with a most tender devotion to Mary in the hearts of her numerous children.

The third child, Robert, was the most outstanding of all. Being most sincere by nature, he never told the least lie. Vivacious and exuberant from childhood, he gave promise of the great things to which God was calling him. He loved piety, purity and innocence of soul, and he guarded these virtues with a profound devotion to the Blessed Virgin. And Mary, who never permits herself to be outdone in generosity, first guided this dear son of hers while he remained in the world, preserving him from every evil. Then, after calling him to the religious life, she led him to the highest summits of sanctity. From his earliest years Robert understood the value of maintaining purity of soul; for this reason he made a solemn vow of virginity to the Queen of Virgins, with all the enthusiasm of youth. He grew up good, obedient and devout, so much so, that mothers pointed him out as a model to their children.

One day in church, after praying fervently in front of the Blessed Virgin's altar, he pointed to some pictures and asked his mother, who was with him, "Mother, who are those men up there?"

"They are Doctors of the Church," she answered.

"And that man in red?"

"He is a Cardinal."

"Well," exclaimed the little boy joyfully, "someday I shall be a Cardinal and a Doctor of the Church, too."

He soon heard Mary's voice inviting him to abandon the world and to consecrate himself to God's service. He resolved to answer generously. In order to succeed he had to overcome the many obstacles placed in his path by his father, but with Mary's help he won out.

When he joined the Jesuits, his great genius and rare virtue attracted so much attention that he was given his degree in philosophy when only twenty-one. He next studied theology at Padua from 1567 to 1569 and at Louvain, where in 1570, he was ordained a Priest. He dedicated himself to preaching and to the teaching of theology.

Recalled to Rome, he placed all his wisdom at the service of the Church and of Christ's Vicar. He held such important posts as Director of the Roman College and Provincial of Naples. As a recompense for all the good he had done for the Church and for the Holy See, Pope Clement VIII made him a Cardinal. He wrote in defense of Mary's Immaculate Conception and she rewarded him by telling him the day of his death.

On September 7, 1621, with the names of Jesus and Mary on his lips, he expired in the arms of the Blessed Virgin, who must have appeared to him at that moment, judging from the radiant smile on his face.

O Mary Immaculate, the dispenser of the treasures of Heaven, I shall always have recourse to you in my sorrows to have peace, in my doubts to have light, in my dangers to be defended, in all my needs to obtain your assistance.

CHAPTER V

THE ANNUNCIATION TO MARY

St. Luke narrates: "Now in the sixth month the Angel Gabriel was sent from God to a town of Galilee called Nazareth, to a Virgin betrothed to a man named Joseph, of the house of David, and the Virgin's name was Mary. And when the Angel had come to her, he said, 'Hail, full of grace, the Lord is with thee. Blessed art thou among women'" (Luke 1: 26-28).

1. **Mary's humility.**—"At the Angel's salutation," writes St. Augustine, "Mary was filled with grace; Eve was cleansed from her guilt; Eve's curse was changed into Mary's blessing. A Virgin became the Mother of God, in order to reconciliate man with God, to give peace to the world, triumph to Heaven, salvation to mankind, and life to the dead. Mary was troubled by the Angel's words and wondered what his salutation could mean." But the Angel added, "Do not be afraid, Mary, for thou hast found grace with God" (Luke 1: 30).

"Ah, do not fear, Mary," comments St. Bernard, "be not astonished if an Angel comes, because He Who is far greater than an Angel will descend to you. How is it that you are surprised at the coming of an Angel, when you have with you the Lord of the Angels? Are you not perhaps worthy of seeing an Angel, when virginity is an angelic life? As proof of this: 'Behold, thou shalt conceive in thy womb,' continued the Angel, 'and shalt bring forth a Son; and thou shalt call His name Jesus' (Luke 1: 31)."

At this point God's messenger paused, respectfully awaiting Mary's reply.

"O Blessed Virgin," exclaims St. Bernard, "the Patriarchs, the Prophets, and the entire world, prostrate at your feet, anxiously await your freeing consent. And not without reason, for the consolation of the afflicted, the redemption of slaves, the freedom of the damned, and the salvation of all the children of Adam and of the entire universe depend upon your word. O incomparable Virgin, give a prompt and affirmative reply. Hasten, O Lady, to utter this word, for Heaven, limbo and earth await your reply, trembling. But what am I saying? The very Lord and King of the universe desires your consent because through this consent He wants to save the world. Heaven, limbo and earth, rejoice and sing—Mary consents! She answers: 'Behold the handmaid of the Lord, be it done to me according to thy word.' At that moment Mary becomes the Spouse and the Mother of God!"

St. Peter Damian writes: "The Word was made flesh. This is what nature admires, the Angel reveres, and man desires; this is what astonishes Heaven, consoles the earth, and troubles hell."

"O profound and wondrous humility of Mary!" cries St. Bonaventure. "An Archangel greets her, tells her that she is full of grace and announces that the Holy Spirit will descend upon her. She sees herself raised to the honored position of God's Mother, she sees herself placed above all creatures, made the Queen of Heaven and earth, yet Mary does not become proud. On the contrary, all this glory is for her nothing but a greater reason for becoming even more admirably humble. She declares 'Behold the handmaid of the Lord' (Luke 1: 38)."

Mary was exalted in proportion to the extent to which she humbled herself. Humility is the secret of sanctity. If Mary had not been humble, the Holy Spirit would not have descended upon her. And if He had not descended upon her, she would not have become the Mother of God. It is clear that if she became God's Mother by the Holy Spirit, God, as she herself affirmed, regarded the humility of His handmaid more than her virginity. O true humility which gave a God to men and life to mortals, which renewed the heavens, purified the earth, opened Paradise, and delivered souls from slavery.

"And therefore let us humble our souls before Him, and continue in a humble spirit, in His service" (Judith 8: 16). We progress in virtue to the extent that we progress in humility.

2. **Mary's purity.**—With her vow of virginity, Mary prevented herself from becoming the Mother

The Annunciation   "Hail, full of grace the Lord is with thee.
Blessed art thou among women" (Luke 1: 26-28).

of the Savior and having the legitimate satisfaction
of loving children. Notwithstanding this, God made
her the greatest of mothers. Mary's purity was so
rare that, according to St. Bernard, it drew down
upon her the pleased gaze of the Lord and made
Him decide to choose her as His Mother. The
apostolate of virgin souls is most efficacious. The
Religious, totally consecrated to God, will become
the mothers of many souls, and the more intense
their love of God, the greater good they will do.

3. **Mary's obedience.**—St. Thomas of Villanova
affirms that Mary never contradicted the Lord, neither in thought, word, nor action. In fact, stripped
of any will of her own, she obeyed God's will always
and in all things. Mary's heart was continuously suf-
fused with the sentiment of submission to the divine
will, as she made clear to the Archangel Gabriel
when he announced to her the plans of the Most
High: "Behold the handmaid of the Lord; be it
done to me according to thy word" (Luke 1: 38).

A Thought from St. Bernard: Behold the Virgin
and the humble one: if you cannot imitate the virginity of the humble one, imitate the humility of the
Virgin. Virginity is a praiseworthy virtue, but humility is a necessary one. The former is advised; the
latter is commanded. You are invited to embrace
virginity but obliged to practice humility. Of virginity it is said, "Let him accept it who can" (Matt.

19: 12). Of humility, instead, it is said, "Whoever does not accept the kingdom of God as a little child will not enter into it" (Mark 10: 15). The former is rewarded, the latter is required. In other words, one can be saved without virginity but not without humility. Humility that weeps over lost virginity can please; but without humility, I dare to say that not even Mary's virginity would have been pleasing.

St. Cyprian

St. Cyprian was converted to Christianity about the year 245 and shortly after, was elected Bishop of Carthage. The change which took place in his way of life was really profound: he almost immediately vowed himself to the practice of chastity and, selling the greater part of his goods, gave what they brought to the poor. He possessed all the true qualities of a man of authority to such a degree that even those not subject to him instinctively bowed to him. He was a true leader in governing the Church entrusted to him. He could show himself condescending at the right times without suffering any loss of authority. Most of his writings are in a pastoral style, and they give a clear idea of his exquisitely practical spirit, which was concerned with all matters, and which showed a happy combination of discretion and strength in ruling over men.

He also wrote many beautiful things on Mary and on the confidence we must have in her. He praised her virginity and called her, "The tree that produced the marvellous Fruit; the house possessed by the Holy Spirit, the door of the Savior, the guarded sanctuary of the Holy Spirit, the abode of Christ's humanity, the house of sanctity which the third Person of the Most Blessed Trinity willed to adorn; the vessel of election in which the Divinity poured the fullness of grace."

During Valerian's persecution, Cyprian was exiled to Curubis on the Mediterranean shore. There he remained a year, continuing to govern his church and to write books.

Recalled to Carthage in September of 258, he was arrested and beheaded in the presence of all his people. In the history of Christianity, St. Cyprian will always remain one of the greatest Bishops.

O most tender Virgin, make us feel the sweetness of your motherly heart, and the might of your intercession with Jesus.

CHAPTER VI

MARY'S VISIT TO ST. ELIZABETH

At the Annunciation, the Angel had told Mary that her cousin Elizabeth had become a mother even though advanced in age. Certain of giving pleasure to her cousin, Mary hastened to go to her, happy to serve her as a devoted handmaid.

"Now in those days Mary arose and went with haste into the hill country, to a town of Juda. And she entered the house of Zachary and saluted Elizabeth. And it came to pass, when Elizabeth heard the greeting of Mary, that the babe in her womb leapt. And Elizabeth was filled with the Holy Spirit, and cried out with a loud voice, saying, 'Blessed art thou among women and blessed is the fruit of thy womb! And how have I deserved that the mother of my Lord should come to me? For behold, the moment that the sound of thy greeting came to my ears, the babe in my womb leapt for joy. And blessed is she who has believed, because the things promised her by the Lord shall be accomplished' " (Luke 1: 39-45).

St. Elizabeth lived in a village lost among the mountains. Although the roads leading to it were hazardous, and the journey there a dangerous one,

Mary set out, repeating with the Prophet Habacuc, "The Lord God is my strength: and He will make my feet like the feet of harts: and He the Conqueror will lead me upon my high places singing Psalms" (3: 19).

Mary went **with haste.** "Learn, O virgins," comments St. Ambrose, "not to stop along the streets or in public squares. Mary, who at home is calm, walks with haste in public. The soul full of the Holy Spirit does not know indulgence nor does it sleep; rather, it runs and flies along the paths of the divine precepts and perfection."

Entering the house of Zachary, Mary greeted Elizabeth: "And she entered the house of Zachary and saluted Elizabeth" (Luke 1: 40).

When Elizabeth heard Mary's greeting, she felt her infant leap in her womb, and she was filled with the Holy Spirit. "And how have I deserved that the mother of my Lord should come to me? . . . And blessed is she who has believed, because the things promised her by the Lord shall be accomplished" (Luke 1: 43-45).

It is almost as though she said: You, Mary, are the woman chosen from all eternity to crush the serpent's head, to give birth to the Divine Word, and to open Heaven. Elizabeth's words are somewhat the same, in certain points, as those of the Angel; therefore, it is evident that she spoke under divine inspiration.

Mary did not delight in these words of praise; she was touched by them and, in a burst of prophetic enthusiasm, she broke forth in the immortal words of the **Magnificat:**

"'My soul magnifies the Lord, and my spirit rejoices in God my Savior; because He has regarded the lowliness of His handmaid; for, behold, henceforth all generations shall call me blessed; because He Who is mighty has done great things for me, and holy is His name; and His mercy is from generation to generation on those who fear Him. He has shown might with His arm, He has scattered the proud in the conceit of their heart. He has put down the mighty from their thrones and has exalted the lowly. He has filled the hungry with good things, and the rich He has sent away empty. He has given help to Israel, His servant, being mindful of His mercy—as He spoke to our fathers—to Abraham and to his posterity forever.' And Mary remained with her about three months and returned to her own house" (Luke 1: 46-56).

Mary's encounter with Elizabeth was the meeting of two great souls, the greeting of two saints. What a fragrance of sanctity, of humility and of fervor rose from this scene of the Visitation! Elizabeth exalts Mary; Mary thanks and exalts the Lord!

1. **Mary's charity.**—Mary was heroic in every virtue, but especially in charity, which she possessed in the highest degree. Mary's heart was an

ocean of charity and of love: she so surpassed the Angels and the Saints in love of God, that it might well be said that even the Seraphim could have descended from Heaven to learn from the heart of Mary how to love God. St. Paul's beautiful praises of charity can all be applied to Mary.

She especially exercised charity in giving us Jesus. Mary brought Jesus into the world. When she entered Elizabeth's house, she brought Jesus there, and with Him, His grace. "And it came to pass, when Elizabeth heard the greeting of Mary, that the babe in her womb leapt. And Elizabeth was filled with the Holy Spirit" (Luke 1: 41).

Mary brought blessings. Following her example, let us try to do good to everyone, where ever we go.

2. **The reverence with which St. Elizabeth welcomed Mary.**—The first to greet Mary was the Angel, who said, "Hail, full of grace, the Lord is with thee. Blessed art thou among women" (Luke 1: 28). The second to greet her was Elizabeth, who added to the angelic salutation these words: "And blessed is the fruit of thy womb" (Luke 1: 42). Fortunate are you, Elizabeth, who have before you the Mother of the Savior, the Queen of Heaven!

From Elizabeth let us learn to love Mary and be devoted to her.

Devotion to the Mother of God is a sure sign of salvation, for she is the Guide, the Queen, the

The Visitation

Mary hastened to go to her cousin Elizabeth,
happy to serve her as a devoted handmaid.

Mother and the Protectress of the elect. Mary never fails to give her faithful devotees abundant grace, help and comfort in order to insure their salvation. He who loves and venerates Mary with filial devotion is infinitely blessed.

3. **Mary's reply to St. Elizabeth.**—Elizabeth glorified Mary by calling her blessed among women, for blessed is the fruit of her womb; she declared herself unworthy of the high honor of welcoming her Lord's Mother in her home. On hearing such praise, Mary attributed everything to God by singing, "My soul magnifies the Lord!" She referred to God, as to the only source of all goodness, the praise given her. It seems as though she meant to say, "You, Elizabeth, exalt the Lord's Mother, but my soul exalts and glorifies God." For this reason, St. Bernard calls the Magnificat, "The exaltation of Mary's humility." This is the song of thanksgiving and of grateful humility. Mary, exalted by St. Elizabeth for her faith and her greatness, and proclaimed the Mother of the Savior, humiliated herself more than ever and proclaimed her nothingness and her weakness, attesting that all that she had came from God.

Like Mary let us also give praise to God: "To ... the one only God, be honor and glory" (1 Tim. 1: 17). May our prayer always be directed first to praising and thanking the Lord. Selfish prayer is less acceptable to God and obtains less fruit.

A Thought from St. Peter Damian: Fortunate Elizabeth! Before her stood the Mother of the Redeemer, the Queen of Heaven; she greeted her sweetly. Even more fortunate, however, was the child she bore in her womb, for he was the first object of this royal visit. Enlightened by the Holy Spirit, he recognized the majesty of the Queen of Angels, who was greeting his mother, and it was given to him to understand the power of that greeting.

St. Pius X

The entire life of this august Pontiff was a hymn of faith and love to Jesus in the Holy Eucharist and to the Blessed Virgin. He was born in Riese on June 2, 1835, and the following day was baptized Joseph.

As a boy Joseph used to go often to the Shrine of *Maria delle Cendrole,* and on Sundays he would bring along his friends. There he would pray devoutly. The Madonna called him to the priesthood, but his parents were poor and could not pay for his studies. Providentially the Patriarch of Venice intervened and granted the boy a scholarship. After his ordination to the priesthood Joseph was appointed a curate in Tombolo, in the diocese of Treviso, where he put into action his zeal for souls.

In 1875 he was elected a Canon of the Cathedral of Treviso and in 1884 Leo XIII consecrated him Bishop of Mantua. It was the third Sunday of Advent, a day set aside to honor the patronage of Mary Immaculate, patroness of Mantua. The fame of the Bishop of Mantua's wisdom and piety grew steadily, and Leo XIII made him a Cardinal and then Patriarch of Venice.

In 1903, the renowned Patriarch of Venice, Cardinal Sarto, was elected Pope and he took the name of Pius X.

The higher this luminous and beneficent star rose, the greater became his manifestations of love for Jesus in the Holy Eucharist and Mary Immaculate. On the occasion of the fiftieth anniversary of the dogma of the Immaculate Conception, Pius X wrote an encyclical on the Madonna: "Ad diem illum," the masterpiece of his devotion to Mary. He describes Mary Most Holy's beauty, her virginity and her influence on humanity; he urges all Christians to be devoted to this good Mother.

One day during an audience granted to some noblemen of Rome, he heard the Angelus ring. At once, he said, "Gentlemen, it is the hour of the Angelus. Will you recite it with me?" An eye witness described him as follows: "I observed him while he prayed. I contemplated the expression on his face, the radiant light in his eyes as he gazed steadily at a picture of the Blessed Virgin. I admired the sweetness of those "Hail Marys" said in such an unusual tone. I was so vividly impressed that I was forced to think: 'Perhaps he sees her.' And I realized then how much we must love the Mother of God."

St. Pius X died on August 20, 1914.

Most glorious Virgin, chosen by God to be the Mother of the eternal Word made flesh, be my guide and counselor in this vale of tears.

CHAPTER VII

THE NATIVITY OF JESUS

The Blessed Virgin stayed at her cousin Elizabeth's house for about three months, serving her as a most humble handmaid. She then returned to Nazareth. As the ninth month after the time of the Angel's message approached, Mary Most Holy and St. Joseph awaited the birth of the Savior of the world with the most profound sentiments of faith, hope and charity.

But it was then that there came an edict from Caesar Augustus that a census of the whole empire should be taken: "Now it came to pass in those days, that a decree went forth from Caesar Augustus that a census of the whole world should be taken. This first census took place while Cyrinus was governor of Syria. And all were going, each to his own town, to register. And Joseph also went from Galilee out of the town of Nazareth into Judea to the town of David, which is called Bethlehem—because he was of the house and family of David—to register together with Mary his espoused wife, who was with child" (Luke 2: 2-5).

Having reached the height of its power, Rome wanted to ascertain the exact number of its subjects.

Palestine, too, being a Roman Province, had to give an account. Joseph imparted the news of the imperial order to his beloved wife. Everyone had to go to the place of origin of his own tribe! Mary and Joseph were descendants of David, who had been born in Bethlehem. Therefore, they would have to go to Bethlehem, the city of their ancestor.

1. **Mary's promptness in obeying the emperor.**—The journey from Nazareth to Bethlehem was a long and hazardous one, and Joseph feared for his wife. But Mary reassured him, saying, "Fear not, the Lord is with us," and they set out. Behold the promptness of the Queen of Heaven in subjecting herself to the commands of her lawful superiors.

2. **The cold reception at Bethlehem.**—Having reached Bethlehem, the holy couple sought lodging in the homes of their relatives and at the public inns, but they could find none. The city was in a turmoil on account of the crowds of strangers flocking from every direction. For the two from Nazareth there was no room! "He came unto His own, and His own received Him not" (John 1: 11).

As a consequence, they were forced to seek shelter outside the city. There were in Palestine many grottoes used by the shepherds to shelter their flocks. It was in one of these that Mary and Joseph took refuge. And in that stable, Mary "brought forth her firstborn Son, and wrapped Him in swaddling clothes, and laid Him in a manger" (Luke 2: 7).

Thus, in the most abject misery, under the rule of Augustus, the long-awaited Messias was born, giving us an admirable example of humility even at the very moment of His birth.

Bethlehem's inhabitants rejected Mary and Joseph, and they humbly went away, without a single complaint or one word of bitterness.

Let us learn to see the world as it is—full of trickery and malice: "The whole world is in the power of the evil one" (1 John 5: 19). Then, we shall not fear the judgments of men nor the world's scorn.

3. **Mary at the manger.**—Who can adequately describe the happiness and tender affection that filled Mary's heart when she first held the Infant Jesus in her arms? What sweet tears she must have shed over Him! What warm kisses! What tender embraces! What loving smiles! What boundless love! "O unique childbirth without pain," exclaims St. Bernard, "unique in purity and freedom from corruption, who will tell of your wonders?"

In the nearby fields shepherds were watching their flocks. And behold, an Angel enveloped in luminous splendor appeared to them to announce the joyful tidings:

"And the Angel said to them, 'Do not be afraid, for behold, I bring you good news of great joy which shall be to all the people; for today in the town of David a Savior has been born to you, Who is Christ the Lord. And this shall be a sign to you: you will find an Infant wrapped in swaddling clothes and lying in a manger.' And suddenly there was with the Angel a multitude of the heavenly host praising God and saying, 'Glory to God in the highest, and on earth peace among men of good will' " (Luke 2: 10-14).

When the Angels disappeared the shepherds said to one another: " 'Let us go over to Bethlehem and see this thing that has come to pass, which the Lord has made known to us.' So they went with haste, and they found Mary and Joseph, and the Babe lying in the manger. And when they had seen, they understood what had been told them concerning this Child. And all who heard marvelled at the things told them by the shepherds. But Mary kept in mind all these things, pondering them in her heart. And the shepherds returned, glorifying and praising God for all that they had heard and seen, even as it was spoken to them" (Luke 2: 15-20).

What a sweet and touching scene! Mary smilingly presented her Son for the shepherds to adore, and explained to them the mysteries upon which the Christian faith rests, the ineffable greatness of the Word of God, and the humility of His Incarnation. Prostrate on the ground with their hands folded, the shepherds listened to her words, adored the Lord, and then returned with joy to their flocks.

In that night a great revelation was made to Mary. On the one hand she understood God's infinite love for men: "For a Child is born to us, and a Son is given to us, and the government is upon His shoulder: and His name shall be called Wonderful, Counsellor, God the Mighty, the Father of the world to come, the Prince of Peace" (Isa. 9: 6). On the other hand, her own passion began at that very moment for she well understood her Son's mission. This was the beginning of her life of adoration, thanksgiving, reparation for our sins, and intense love for Jesus, the God-Man.

Mary is the model of adorers. In the Holy Eucharist we have the same Jesus Who constituted the great delight and love of Mary. As His Mother, let us, too, love Him and pray to Him.

A Thought from St. Peter Chrysologus: In the presence of God, Heaven is frightened, the Angels quake, the creature staggers, and nature faints, but a mere maiden received this God within herself and so pleased Him with the hospitality she offered Him that she merited and obtained, by reason of the dwelling place which she provided for Him, peace on earth, glory in Heaven, salvation for sinners, life for the dead, friendship between Heaven and earth, and intimacy between God and men.

The Council of Ephesus

Ephesus is the city of Mary because it was her abode for a few years, and because at Ephesus the dogma that Mary is truly the Mother of God was defined.

It was the year 431. Nestorius, Patriarch of Constantinople, was persisting in his heresy, in spite of repeated reprimands, and denying that the Blessed Virgin is the Mother of God. Pope St. Celestine I condemned the heresy and convened the great Ecumenical Council at which St. Cyril presided. The council opened on June twenty-second of the same year, and more than two hundred Bishops participated in it. Having carefully examined the doctrine held by Nestorius, they condemned it as being heretical and impious; then they proclaimed the Catholic doctrine concerning the unity of the person of Jesus Christ and the Divine Motherhood of the Blessed Virgin. This doctrine was confirmed and subscribed to by all the Fathers of the council. The people waiting expectantly in the public square jubilantly hailed the Fathers and, with blazing torches, conducted them to their homes. The whole city was illuminated, and everyone celebrated joyously the triumph of the truth, the glory of Christ and of the Virgin Mary declared the Mother of God.

I venerate you, O Virgin most holy, as the Mother of the only-begotten Son, and I consecrate to you all my soul with all its powers, my body with all its senses, and my heart with all its affections.

CHAPTER VIII

THE ADORATION OF THE MAGI

With great joy, Mary had watched the shepherds render homage to the Infant Jesus. However, besides the shepherds, who were humble and simple people, great and learned men also came to adore the Infant. Jesus willed to call to Himself even the pagans, because He had come upon the earth for all men without any distinction of class or nationality. Mary saw the Magi, who had come from the Orient, kneel before Jesus, acknowledging His sovereignty.

1. **The arrival of the Magi in Bethlehem.**—The following is St. Matthew's account: "Now when Jesus was born in Bethlehem of Judea, in the days of King Herod, behold Magi came from the East to Jerusalem, saying, 'Where is He that is born King of the Jews? For we have seen His star in the East and have come to worship Him.' But when King Herod heard this, he was troubled, and so was all Jerusalem with him. And gathering together all the chief priests and Scribes of the people, he inquired of them where the Christ was to be born. And they said to him, 'In Bethlehem of Judea; for thus it is written by the prophet: And thou, Bethlehem, of

the land of Juda, art by no means least among the princes of Juda; for from thee shall come forth a leader Who shall rule My people Israel.' Then Herod summoned the Magi secretly, and carefully ascertained from them the time when the star had appeared to them. And sending them to Bethlehem, he said, 'Go and make careful inquiry concerning the Child, and when you have found Him, bring me word, that I too may go and worship Him.' Now they, having heard the king, went their way. And behold, the star that they had seen in the East went before them, until it came and stood over the place where the Child was. And when they saw the star they rejoiced exceedingly. And entering the house, they found the Child with Mary His Mother, and falling down they worshipped Him. And opening their treasures they offered Him gifts of gold, frankincense and myrrh" (Matt. 2: 1-11).

History does not tell us who these Magi were—whether they were kings or wise men, whether they were three or more, or what their names were. Tradition, however, says that they were kings, from Arabia, and it even gives their names: Melchior, Gaspar, Balthasar.

After the humble folk, the shepherds, there came to the manger, the great and the powerful—great men who yet knew how to humble themselves.

When they reached the grotto, the star disappeared. There at the grotto was Mary—the **morning**

Nativity of Jesus

"And she brought forth her firstborn Son,
and wrapped Him in swaddling clothes,
and laid Him in a manger" (Luke 2: 7).

star, who appeared then in all her splendor. Mantled in virtue and sanctity, she came forth from the shadows and, presenting the Infant Jesus, said, "This is my Son."

2. **During their visit to Bethlehem the Magi learned the entire Gospel and left the grotto transformed into saints and apostles.**—They presented to the Virgin their gifts for Jesus: gold, frankincense and myrrh. Mary obtained for them an increase of wisdom and charity, an increase of piety and devotion, love of mortification, and of pure and holy living.

According to tradition, when the Magi returned to their own land they won many souls to Christ. They were steadfast in persecution, they spread devotion to Mary, and they shed their blood for Jesus Christ. Their bodies were transported to Constantinople, then to Milan and, finally, to Cologne, where today they are still preserved and honored.

3. **The Magi found Jesus through Mary.**— The Evangelist writes: "And entering the house, they found the Child with Mary His Mother" (Matt. 2: 11).

Having reached their destination, they found Him upon Whom their faith rested, but it was Mary who brought them to know Jesus, who showed Him to them and presented Him for them to adore. The

Gospel does not describe the graces which flooded the souls of the Magi at that time, but undoubtedly they were numerous. From Mary they learned the mystery of the Incarnation, and for this reason, they adored Jesus. In return, they received so many spiritual gifts, so much enlightenment, consolation and celestial fervor that they desired labor, weariness, suffering, and death for Jesus Christ.

Mary is the great apostle who brings Jesus to the world. An apostle is a person who bears such a great love for God that his heart cannot contain it and thus he feels the need of diffusing it and implanting it in others. The apostle is animated by the spirit of Jesus Christ, and he wants to conquer every soul for Him.

Mary, Mother, Teacher and Queen of the Apostles, presented her Jesus not only to the Hebrews but also to the pagans.

As Mary, let us make Jesus loved by many souls, with whatever form of apostolate is open to us. In the encyclical "Summi Pontificatus," Pope Pius XII says: "The prayer of the Church to the Lord of the Harvest that He send laborers into His vineyard, has been answered in a way suited to our present-day needs. The lay apostolate supplements and completes the often insufficient energies of the sacerdotal apostolate. A fervent band of men, women, boys, and girls obedient to the voice of the Supreme Shepherd and to the directives of their

Bishops, consecrate themselves with the full ardor of their souls to the works of the apostolate, in order to bring back to Christ the masses of people who have separated themselves from Him."

This apostolic labor, performed according to the spirit of the Church, almost consecrates the layman to the **ministry of Christ** in the sense which St. Augustine thus explains: "O Brethren, when you hear the Lord say: Wherever I am, there also is My minister, you must not only think in terms of His good Bishops and Priests. In your own way, you too, must be ministers of Christ by leading good lives, by giving alms, by preaching His name and doctrine to whomever you can. All of you should do this. The father of a family, for example, must realize the duty that is his—by the very fact that he is a father—to love his family paternally. For Christ and for eternal life, let him instruct, exhort, reprimand, discipline and show kindness to his loved ones; so that in his own home he may exercise the function of the Priest and in a certain respect even of the Bishop, serving Christ in order to be with Him in eternity."

Pius IX

The name of this august Pontiff cannnot be separated from the name of the Blessed Virgin Mary, to whom he was greatly devoted. In 1854, he solemnly proclaimed and defined, from the immovable rock of the Vatican, the dogma of Mary's Immaculate Conception—a dogma which, four

Proclamation of the Dogma of the Immaculate Conception   Podesti - Anderson

Pope Pius IX solemnly proclaimed and defined,
from the immovable rock of the Vatican,
the dogma of Mary's Immaculate Conception.

years later, the Virgin herself deigned to confirm to the humble Bernadette Soubirous in the grotto of Massabielle.

Mary carried out a special mission in regard to her beloved devotee. She protected him in the midst of every danger. She made him strong and fearless. She formed him after her own heart, instilling in him all those sentiments of charity, love and compassion by which a father, an apostle, and a saint must be inspired.

Born in times which were very sorrowful for the Church, when it seemed as though the gates of hell would prevail, and Peter's boat would perish beneath the waves, this future Pope entrusted himself to Mary from his earliest years. And the Blessed Virgin, who was watching over him, led him into the priesthood, helping him to overcome very great difficulties. In 1828, Pope Leo XII elected him Archbishop of Spoleto; Pope Gergory XVI, admiring his zeal and sanctity, transferred him to Imola so that there, too, he might restore the state of the Church as he had done in Spoleto. In a short time these two dioceses rose to a new life and splendor. His pastoral activities in these two dioceses were such that he was believed to be another St. Charles Borromeo or another St. Francis, and some, upon seeing him, exclaimed, "There goes our future Pope." And they were not mistaken.

His superior gifts and tireless zeal so impressed Gregory XVI that he made him a Cardinal in 1839. He was then forty-eight. A few years later he ascended the throne of Peter.

Finally he was able to make known to the whole world his filial affection for the Blessed Virgin; at last the time had arrived to declare as an article of faith that which Christians of all centuries had always believed: the Immaculate Conception of the Blessed Virgin Mary. He zealously sought to make devotion to the most holy Mother of God grow in men's hearts. He exhorted, encouraged and invited everyone by his own example to have recourse to Mary. And this ardent enthusiasm of his for devotion to

Mary merited for him the singular protection of his heavenly Patroness. It was Mary who gave him strength and courage to withstand all persecutions, and when in 1848, the revolution forced him to flee to Gaeta, his sole comforts were the Holy Eucharist, Which he carried with him, and his complete trust in Mary's powerful help.

On February 7, 1878, he took his flight to Heaven after exclaiming, "Mother of mercy, protect us from our enemies and receive us in the hour of our death."

Oh, holy Mary, convert me, and obtain for me the grace to love Jesus Christ above all things and to console you also by living a holy life, in order that one day I may be able to see you in Heaven.

CHAPTER IX

THE PRESENTATION OF JESUS IN THE TEMPLE

Eight days after the birth of Jesus, Mary, diligent observer of the Law, presented the Divine Infant for the ceremony of circumcision by which a Hebrew infant was officially enrolled in Judaism and declared a legitimate son of Abraham, to whom God had said, "And thou therefore shalt keep My covenant, and thy seed after thee in their generations. This is My covenant which you shall observe, between Me and you, and thy seed after thee: All the male kind of you shall be circumcised" (Gen. 17: 9-10).

In imitation of Abraham, who circumcised his own child, the infant's father personally performed the ceremony at home, reciting the prescribed blessing. The whole family and the neighbors attended and welcomed "the one who entered the alliance." Regarding circumcision, Jesus obeyed His heavenly Father, and He, more appropriately than David, could exclaim, "Sacrifice and oblation Thou didst not desire; but thou hast pierced ears for Me. Burnt offering and sin offering Thou didst not require: then said I, Behold I come" (Ps. 39, 7-8).

By nature Jesus was not subject to this law, but He willed to submit Himself to it, so as to give us an example of obedience. It was then that the Name of Jesus was given to Him, as the Angel had said even before He was conceived in His Mother's womb.

Mary wanted to observe another law even though she was not required to do so by reason of her position, unique in the world, as a Virgin Mother. According to the law of Moses, forty days after giving birth to a child, every woman was obliged to go to the Temple for her purification. Furthermore, if the child was her first-born, it had to be consecrated to the Lord.

The law specified that for the poor, the offering of two turtledoves or two pigeons was sufficient. When forty days had passed, Mary went to the Temple for the double ceremony of purification and presentation. What an example of humility! The Gospel explicitly narrates the event: "And when the days of her purification were fulfilled according to the Law of Moses, they took Him up to Jerusalem to present Him to the Lord—as it is written in the Law of the Lord, 'Every male that opens the womb shall be called holy to the Lord'— and to offer a sacrifice according to what is said in the Law of the Lord, 'a pair of turtledoves or two young pigeons'" (Luke 2: 22-24).

And the Virgin Mother fulfilled the offering of her Son. The offering was accepted and was to be consummated on Calvary.

A venerable old man, Simeon by name, just and devout, was awaiting the consolation of Israel. The Holy Spirit was in him and had revealed to him that he would not die before seeing the Christ of the Lord. Led by the Holy Spirit, he went to the Temple. Yielding to his desires, Mary placed the Divine Infant in his arms. Simeon took Him, contemplated Him with ardent love, and enthusiastically exclaimed: "Now Thou dost dismiss Thy servant, O Lord, according to Thy word, in peace; because my eyes have seen Thy salvation, which Thou hast prepared before the face of all peoples: a light of revelation to the Gentiles, and a glory for Thy people Israel" (Luke 2: 29-32).

Mary and Joseph were greatly impressed: how did Simeon know the secret of the Messias? Suddenly, however, the holy man interrupted his blessing and his face grew troubled. He turned to the young Mother and said: "Behold, this Child is destined for the fall and for the rise of many in Israel, and for a sign which shall be contradicted. And thy own soul a sword shall pierce, that the thoughts of many hearts may be revealed" (Luke 2: 34-35). What an impression these words must have made on Mary's soul! From that moment on,

Presentation

*"And when the days of her purification were fulfilled
according to the Law of Moses,
they took Him up to Jerusalem to present Him to the Lord."*

always before her eyes was a vision of persecutions, calumny, anxieties, agony and death.

The elderly prophetess Anna, daughter of Phanuel, of the tribe of Aser, was also present at this scene, for she worshipped in the Temple night and day, with fastings and prayers. Enlightened from on high, she also echoed Simeon's canticle glorifying God, speaking of Jesus "to all who were awaiting the redemption of Jerusalem" (Luke 2: 38).

Let us consider the relations between Mary and Jesus, and let us learn the relations which must exist between the faithful and priests. Mary is the Mother of the great and unique Priest; all other priests share in the priesthood of Jesus. In Holy Mass the priest says, **"This is My Body,"** precisely because Jesus speaks through him.

What were Mary's relations with Jesus the Priest? She begot Him, nourished Him, educated Him, and offered Him to God. She assisted at His sacrifice on Calvary. Not only for Jesus was this tender care of Mary's but also for all His Apostles and disciples.

From our heavenly Mother let us learn to revere and respect priests. St. Francis of Assisi says: "I shall always honor the priest who gives me the Body and Blood of Jesus, and communicates God's word to me." By honoring priests one honors Jesus, Whose ministers they are: "Let a man so account us as servants of Christ and stewards of the mysteries of God" (I Cor. 4: 1). "He who hears you, hears Me; and he who rejects you, rejects Me" (Luke 10: 16).

The priest is another Jesus Christ; therefore one must have a supernatural concept of him. St. Teresa asserted that she would willingly kiss the ground upon which a priest walked. St. Francis de Sales, assisting at the ordination ceremony of a deacon saw his Guardian Angel, who had been at his right, cross to his left after the ordination, as if out of respect for the priestly character. And St. Augustine, to show that the priest is truly another Christ, said: "Is it Peter who baptizes? It is Jesus Who baptizes. Is it Judas who baptizes? It is Jesus Who baptizes."

Let us always have great respect for priests and pray for them. Let us also pray for vocations to the priesthood and help them as much as possible.

It is everyone's duty to co-operate in forming priests, for everyone receives from the priest supernatural life, pardon, Holy Communion and the Gospel.

A Thought from St. Gregory: Treasure in your mind the word of God that you receive from the preacher's mouth, for the word of God is the soul's nourishment.

St. Bonaventure

From his tenderest years St. Bonaventure had a devotion to Mary, and this devotion grew steadily. Keeping his eyes on this divine star, he let himself be guided by her in all things, certain that with Mary helping him, he would always be successful.

Elected Superior General of the Franciscans, he placed the Order under Mary's special protection and propagated her devotion among its members.

St. Bonaventure is rightly numbered among Mary's greatest devotees. In praise of Mary he wrote a commentary on the Hail, Holy Queen and composed a hymn on the style of the Te Deum.

Impressed by Bonaventure's virtues, Pope Gregory X made him a Cardinal in June, 1273, and named him Bishop of Albano. Shortly after participating in the Council of Lyon, he died.

In 1482 he was canonized a Saint, and in 1587 he was proclaimed a Doctor of the Church by Pope Sixtus V.

I grieve for you, O Mary most sorrowful, in the affliction of your tender heart at the prophecy of the holy and aged Simeon. Dear Mother, by your heart so afflicted, obtain for me the virtue of humility and the gift of the holy fear of God.

CHAPTER X

THE FLIGHT INTO EGYPT

Perhaps the Magi had informed Mary how Herod had advised them to go to Bethlehem to seek the Infant and then return to tell him where they had found Him that he, too, might pay homage to the newborn Child. Mary probably knew Herod, but she reassured herself with the word of God: "The Lord is my light and my salvation, whom should I fear? The Lord is the protector of my life: of whom shall I be afraid?" (Ps. 26: 1).

And God intervened to thwart Herod's wicked plans. He warned the Magi, in a marvelous manner, during their sleep, not to return to Herod They obeyed and went back to their country without passing through Jerusalem again.

The Infant Jesus would have to be taken to Egypt for safety. The Gospel narrates the event clearly and briefly as follows: "But when they had departed, behold, an Angel of the Lord appeared in a dream to Joseph, saying, 'Arise, and take the Child and His Mother, and flee into Egypt, and remain there until I tell thee. For Herod will seek the Child to destroy Him.' So he arose, and took the Child and His Mother by night, and withdrew into Egypt, and remained there until the death of Herod; that what was spoken by the Lord through the prophet might be fulfilled, 'Out of Egypt I called My Son' " (Matt. 2: 13-15).

We can readily surmise that the holy fugitives undertook their journey in the direst poverty. Tradition has been pleased to picture Mary sitting on the donkey holding the Child Jesus in her arms, while St. Joseph walked along beside them.

During that long, weary journey, they spoke little, being absorbed in deep thought, and in prayer.

It was the triumph of tyranny over innocence, weakness, and sanctity. Herod abused his power; he employed deceit and cruelty—all because he jealously feared a future rival in the newborn Child.

The Holy Family humbly bowed to the will of the Celestial Father. They submitted themselves to the grave difficulties of exile. Thus God's prophecies and designs were fulfilled.

Emigrants, exiles from their homeland, venerate Jesus, Mary and Joseph in their flight and in their stay in Egypt: the land of exile. There are those who leave their country out of a desire for adventure or money, or in order to study, or because duty calls them. More numerous, however, are those who are forced to leave because they cannot earn a decent living in their own land.

These emigrants must patiently resign themselves to God's will, but they should also find

Flight into Egypt

St. Joseph arose, and took the Child and His Mother by night, and withdrew into Egypt, and remained there until the death of Herod.

charity and understanding everywhere. Life often holds moments of darkness and uncertainty, but whoever abandons himself to the will of God will be protected and defended.

"Then Herod, seeing that he had been tricked by the Magi, was exceedingly angry; and he sent and slew all the boys in Bethlehem and all its neighborhood who were two years old or under, according to the time that he had carefully ascertained from the Magi. Then was fulfilled what was spoken through Jeremias the prophet, 'A voice was heard in Rama weeping and loud lamentation; Rachel weeping for her children, and she would not be comforted, because they are no more' " (Matt. 2: 16-18).

Where did the Holy Family live during the stay in Egypt? The exact place is not known.

How long did this exile last? Certainly not many years, for it is known that their return took place immediately after the death of Herod, and it was only a few years after his heinous crime, that Herod died, eaten by remorse and by worms. Then the Angel of the Lord appeared in a dream to Joseph and said: " 'Arise, and take the Child and His Mother, and go into the land of Israel, for those who sought the Child's life are dead.' So he arose and took the Child and His Mother, and went into the land of Israel. But hearing that Archelaus was reigning in Judea in place of his father Herod, he was afraid to go there; and being warned in a dream, he withdrew into the region of Galilee. And he went and settled in a town called Nazareth; that there might be fulfilled what was spoken through the prophets, 'He shall be called a Nazarene' " (Matt. 2: 20-23).

Let us admire Mary's docile obedience to the Divine Will. In such a crushing trial Mary's faith did not falter in the least, nor was there any decrease in her total abandon to God's will. Let us learn to trust in God. He abandons no one, and if He sometimes asks for sacrifices, it is always for our spiritual benefit.

A Thought from St. Thomas of Villanova: This faithful handmaid, Mary, never contradicted the Lord in deed or thought; she was obedient to the Divine will always and in all things.

Dante Alighieri

Dante was born in a century of great devotion to Mary, a century when masterpieces of art in her honor abounded.

Dante's devotion to Mary, nourished from early childhood, increased with the training he received from the Franciscans and Dominicans, and was deepened by his study of Sacred Scripture and the Church Fathers. From St. Bonaventure he learned to imitate Mary in every action. From St. Bernard, he learned to love the praises, the invocations, the aspirations, the sighs and bursts of love, the most tender, ardent sentiments of a lover of Mary, and these he later sprinkled throughout his poem. Dante's devotion to Mary was translated into the most beautiful and sublime expression that literary form has produced.

The Divine Comedy is primarily of moral-religious significance: it treats of leaving the paths of evil, purifying oneself and freeing oneself from evil so as to be worthy of the Beatific Vision and earn eternal life. But how does one abandon evil? Conversion is a work which can only be accomplished with Heaven's special help. This help comes to us through Mary, our sweet Mother, the refuge of sinners, the Mother of mercy, the Mother of divine grace.

Dante confessed his love for Mary.

Dear Mother, by your heart so troubled during the flight into Egypt and your sojourn there, obtain for me the virtue of generosity, especially towards the poor, and the gift of piety.

CHAPTER XI

THE LOSING AND FINDING OF JESUS

The boy Jesus was advancing in grace before God and men, in the little home of Nazareth with Mary, His Mother and Joseph, His foster-father: "And Jesus advanced in wisdom and age and grace before God and men" (Luke 2: 52). Mary regarded with great delight this her Son, "beautiful above the sons of men" (Ps. 44: 3), the most modest, the best and most affectionate. Oh, fortunate Mother! With her she had that Son whose boyhood was a wonder of beauty and goodness. Jesus worked with His foster-father and received a fitting education.

As soon as He reached the age of twelve, the Boy Jesus was taken to Jerusalem for the feast of the Passover. At that age, in fact, a Hebrew boy became a son of the Law, responsible for his own acts. For the first time, on the sabbath, he was called before the sacred volumes of the Law to bless the Eternal God for having chosen the Hebrew people as the custodian of His Law. Therefore, Mary had the joy of witnessing this entrance of Jesus into the Temple of Jerusalem. A sorrowful episode occurred, however, which reminded her that her Son was destined for a mission that demanded painful separations.

After the seven days of the feast were over, Mary and Joseph started out on their return trip, but Jesus remained in Jerusalem without their noticing it. On the day of departure all was a turmoil of shouting men, of guides rushing here and there, of caravans setting forth. With great difficulty groups banded together and set out on the journey. After a few miles, however, the first stop was made for needed rest. It was then that family members reunited, and Mary and Joseph succeeded in finding one another. As their glances met, their hearts began to beat fearfully; silence sealed their lips, and the same question shook them immediately: Where was Jesus? Anxiously they hurried from group to group. Neither relatives nor friends, however, had seen their Son. Perhaps Jesus was somewhere with friends met at the feast. He would appear at any moment. . . . But night fell and Jesus did not arrive! Trembling in anguish, Mary and Joseph returned to Jerusalem in search of their treasure. They questioned the city guards, the women going to the fountain, the porters and beggars, but no one had seen their Son. Finally, after three days of searching, they found Him in the Temple seated among the doctors, listening to them and asking them questions, while "all who were listening to Him were amazed at His understanding and His answers" (Luke 2: 47).

The Blessed Virgin stopped and so did Joseph. They would have liked to rush to Him, embrace Him, and kiss Him, but something mysterious restrained them. They had searched for Him in mortal anguish, believing that He too was searching for them. Instead, they found Him occupied with other matters, as though He had no need of them! He was seated among the doctors of the Law, listening to them and questioning them, filling them with wonder at His discerning questions and wise answers. The sorrowful Mary called out to Him, exclaiming: "Son, why hast Thou done so to us? Behold, in sorrow Thy father and I have been seeking Thee." Calmly and serenely, Jesus replied: "How is it that you sought Me? Did you not know that I must be about My Father's business?" (Luke 2: 48-49).

Before Joseph, whom Mary called the father of Jesus, the heavenly Boy referred to His other Father, His true Father, and to His inscrutable rights. He had come into the world to do His Father's will and to save mankind: "I have come down from Heaven, not to do My own will, but the will of Him Who sent Me" (John 6: 38).

Not yet understanding the entire greatness of the mission entrusted to Jesus, Mary "kept all these things carefully in her heart" (Luke 2: 51).

With His example, Jesus taught that for love of God's Kingdom we must know how to detach ourselves from our parents and all those whom we love. "And He went down with them and came to Nazareth, and was subject to them" (Luke 2: 51).

There are many lessons which could be reaped from this episode: the choice of one's vocation, the search for Jesus when one loses Him through sin, and obedience to the Heavenly Father. We shall mention, however, one thing only: in life there are many mysterious events—events that God permits for our good, for our spiritual progress. There is progress and retrogression, fervor and discouragement and even painful falls, because of which some souls exclaim, "But why, O Jesus, do You permit this?"—just as Mary said, "My Son, why have you done so to us?" In such circumstances we must love Jesus, love Him deeply and believe that what happens, happens because of a divine disposition, and that it is for our own good. Let us fear ourselves, and confide in God, trusting in His divine grace. When Jesus enriches us with benefits and attracts us, let us think that it is grace working in us. When we are tempted, let us think that it is our own frailty. Let us humble ourselves, for our part, and let us elevate ourselves on high, through union with Jesus. We must not expect our reward upon this earth: God permits so much suffering so as to offer us opportunities for gaining merits.

Let us think of what we would have liked to have done when we are at the point of death.

Let us choose that which costs us the most: these are precious rules for successfully overcoming life's obstacles and difficulties.

A Thought from St. Bernard: In dangers, in difficulties and in trials, think of Mary, call on Mary. May her name always be on your lips; may it always be engraved upon your heart.

St. Alphonsus Rodriguez

One of Mary's greatest devotees was St. Alphonsus Rodriguez.

On July 25, 1531, Alphonsus was born in Segovia, an industrial and commercial city of old Castile. As a child he showed his devotion to Mary, a devotion which ever increased with the passing of the years. After a somewhat turbulent life, he recognized, in his trials, God's voice calling him to the Jesuits, and he answered promptly. He repented of his past life and armed himself with the powerful weapons of penance and prayer. And Mary showed him, even in a tangible way, how much this pleased her.

When his two years as a novice were completed in a most exemplary manner, Alphonsus was permitted to take his vows in religion. He made it a practice to honor the Blessed Virgin by the daily recitation of the Rosary, of the Office of the Immaculate, of the Litany, of twelve Hail Holy Queens, and twelve Hail Marys, with the intention of sanctifying the hours of the day and night.

The Hail Mary became as his breath, his most spontaneous ejaculation, so much so that after his death they discovered that the thumb and index finger of his right hand were calloused from his continuous fingering of the beads. Furthermore, he had made a pact with his Guardian Angel to the effect that while he slept, the Angel would recite the Hail Mary, so that the salutation to his Queen would not cease.

He progressed daily in the virtues of prayer and of mortification. These virtues led him to the highest and continuous union with God so that, at times, just by saying, "Lord," or "My Beloved is with me and I am with Him," he would become rapt in ecstasy.

However, that which made of Alphonsus a hero and martyr were the great temptations with which the Lord tried him, and which he, as a valiant soldier, successfully overcame.

Alphonsus' *zeal* for the salvation of souls was immense. He prayed incessantly for the missionaries and preachers of his Society.

His writings, full of great love of God, were also the instruments of his zeal.

After a life expanded for the Lord and after an ecstasy of three consecutive days, Alphonsus flew to his "Loves" as he habitually called Jesus and Mary, pronouncing their adorable Names for the last time. On January 15, 1888, Pope Leo XIII numbered him among the Saints, the reward promised to all who are devoted to Mary.

O Virgin most pure, by your motherly heart so full of anguish at the loss of your dear Jesus, obtain for me the virtue of chastity and the gift of knowledge.

CHAPTER XII

MARY AT NAZARETH

Heaven is the principal and ultimate end of our life. "This is the will of God, your sanctification" (1 Tim. 4: 3). We must sanctify our daily life as Mary, our sublime model, sanctified her whole life on earth. Mary walked in the ways of God in an irreproachable manner.

Already up at the cock's crow, Mary would bake bread, go to the fountain, cook for her family, spin, weave, wash clothes at the nearby stream and mend robes and blankets for the poor as it is written: "And stretch out thy hand to the poor, that thy expiation and thy blessing may be perfected. A gift hath grace in the sight of all the living, and restrain not grace from the dead. Be not wanting in comforting them that weep, and walk with them that mourn. Be not slow to visit the sick: for by these things thou shalt be confirmed in love" (Ecclus. 7: 36-39).

In thought let us enter the little home in Nazareth where lived the holiest family; let us try to lift the veil that conceals Mary's intimate life from us. Let us illumine our mind with the light of faith and the warmth of devotion. How was Mary's life at Nazareth? It was a simple, ordered life, which the Angels of Heaven might have envied. Externally the life that the Madonna led for thirty years within the walls of her home in Nazareth, was ordinary. By virtue of its sanctity, however, it was exceptional.

Mary's life in Nazareth can be summarized in three words: it was a life of prayer, work and humble charity.

1. **A life of prayer**—Mary's heart was like a perpetually burning censer because of its fragrance; it resembled a perpetually shining lamp because of its light of the most fervent and incessant prayer. Who can describe Mary's prayer? She devoted herself to mental prayer, vocal prayer and vital prayer. Mary meditated the Sacred Scripture, read it often and preserved its words in her heart. She understood the Scripture well, as is seen in her **Magnificat**. Mary had formed her style from Sacred Scripture, from which she drew food for her faith and nourishment for her piety. She was always absorbed in God and reflecting on the divine mysteries.

Besides mental prayer, Mary practised vocal prayer which is so acceptable to God and so meritorious. She recited and sang the psalms with a fevor that was more than seraphic. She revealed to St. Elizabeth of Hungary: "I always arose in the heart of the night to pray. With great ardor I begged the Lord my God to grant me humility, patience, good-

Mary at Nazareth   Gagliardi-Alinari

*Mary's life was a living prayer because
her actions were the most perfect that can be conceived.*

ness, sweetness and all other virtues necessary to render me worthy and pleasing in His sight. I also begged Him to allow me to see the time in which would live the Virgin who was to give birth to the Son of God. I asked Him to preserve my sight that I might contemplate her, my tongue that I might praise her, my hands that I might serve her, and my knees that I might adore in her womb the Son of God."

What can be said, moreover, of the prayers she offered in union with Jesus and Joseph?

Mary also practised vital prayer. This third type of prayer is defined by theologians as: a good deed offered to God with the intention of obtaining some benefit from Him. We know that every good action has a triple value: meritorious, impetratory, and reparatory. Mary offered God the reparatory value of her good works that He might have mercy on poor sinners. She offered Him the impetratory value for His glory and the salvation of souls. The meritorious value, instead, being personal, could not be ceded to anyone but steadily increased her merits.

Mary's life was a living prayer because her actions were the most perfect that can be conceived: from the simplest domestic tasks to the noblest acts of prayer and contemplation. The little house of Nazareth was thus the greatest Temple and Shrine that ever existed, for Jesus, Mary and Joseph lived there and God received from there the greatest praise and the most beautiful prayers that ever reached His throne.

Does our prayer resemble Mary's? Let us ask for the grace to attain to constant union with God, to pray well always, and to make all our actions a hymn of praise to the Most Blessed Trinity.

2. **A life of work.**—A condition willed for all men by God in the earthly Paradise was: "In the sweat of thy face thou shalt eat bread" (Gen. 3: 19). These words not only proclaim a curse and condemnation but a strict obligation to work imposed on all men as a means of penance and expiation: "If any man will not work, neither let him eat" (2 Thess. 3: 10). Thus, work is not only a natural precept but also a divine precept: Jesus Christ Himself gave us the example regarding work. And Mary, Christ's most perfect imitator, imitated Him also in work. In the little house of Nazareth, Mary led a life of incessant labor, of total dedication to her duty, and of sacrifice. By herself she took care of the domestic tasks, by herself she saw to the order and cleanliness of the house, and by herself she prepared the daily meal for Jesus and Joseph. What an example for us! Let us, too, sanctify our lives with constant, unceasing labor and daily fidelity to our duties. "Let us work, let us work," St. Joseph Benedict Cottolengo used to say, "we shall rest in

heaven!" The tireless Apostle, St. Paul said, "While we have time, let us do good" (Gal. 6: 10).

3. **A life of humble charity.**—St. Anselm writes: "The more a heart is pure and devoid of self, the more it will be filled with love for God and neighbor." No one surpassed Mary's purity and humility. Therefore, she surpassed the love of all men and Angels for God and for souls, too, for it is impossible to love God without loving one's neighbor, the living image of God. Mary's heart was an ocean of charity and love. "Mary's soul was so smitten by divine love," writes St. Bernard, "that she perfectly fulfilled the greatest commandment, and she could very well exclaim: 'I to my beloved, and my beloved to me' (Cant. 6: 2)."

God, Who is love, came on earth to enkindle in all the flame of divine love, but He inflamed no heart as much as His mother's which, free from earthly affections, was made to burn with this sacred fire. Mary's heart was a veritable blazing furnace of divine love—a furnace whose flames took two directions: one towards God, and the other towards her neighbor. "Indeed, whoever loves God," says St. Thomas, "loves everything God loves." And God loves man with infinite love. Thus Mary also loved all men with a most tender love. Moreover, among all those who constitute "our neighbor," we must give first preference to those who are nearest us, with whom we share the joys and sorrows of daily life. Therefore, Mary's love was poured forth first of all upon Jesus and St. Joseph.

We must not think that the little home at Nazareth was exempt from every sorrow. Even there, the Lord permitted sorrow to enter, so that the members of the Holy Family might sanctify themselves more and more, and we might receive the example of charity and patience so as to practice St. Paul's saying: "Bear one another's burdens, and so you will fulfill the law of Christ" (Gal. 6: 2).

Let us contemplate Mary's patience, humility and retirement.

Mary was **patient.** She underwent many sufferings, but always with complete resignation to God's Will. She suffered when she could offer her Divine Son nothing but poor swaddling clothes. She suffered when she presented Him to the Temple and heard the aged Simeon's prophecy: "And thy own soul a sword shall pierce" (Luke 2: 35). She suffered when she brought him across the desert into a land of infidels, in order to escape the fury of an early persecution. She suffered when she wiped the sweat from His brow, when she heard the Pharisees' threats and the people's vile accusations. She suffered when, standing at the foot of the cross, she saw her beloved Son die amid a sea of sorrows.

Mary was **humble.** This beautiful virtue was unknown to the world: Jesus came down from Heaven to teach it with His example and Mary was His first and most perfect imitator. Humility is the way to Heaven, the secret for reaching the throne of glory, the sweet fragrance which captivates God and leads Him to pour into the souls of those who possess it the vivifying waters of grace. Mary was the most humble creature. No one has been more exalted than she, for no one has humbled himself more than she.

Furthermore, Mary loved **retirement** and solitude. She spoke little, never displayed herself in public, avoided the world, and sought God alone. Her words were always courteous and directed to God's glory and the good of souls. What an intimate union with God was hers!

May silence, humility, patience and charity be our everyday virtues. In imitation of the Blessed Virgin, we shall sanctify our days.

A Thought from St. Ambrose: Think of how great Mary was, and yet when she was sought, she was found in no other place but her own room.

May she show you how to conduct yourself.

Solitude teaches modesty, and retirement is the school of reserve.

St. Joan of Arc

This heroine was born of devout parents in the year 1412, in Lorraine. From early childhood she had a tender devotion to Mary and a great trust in her patronage. Her young years were spent in the occupations of a simple life; she tended the sheep and prayed constantly. The Queen of Heaven, who had great plans for this girl, consoled her with frequent visions and prepared her to save France as a maiden warrior.

Obedient to the mysterious voices that came to her from on high, Joan presented herself to the king of France, Charles VII, who believed in the girl's divine inspirations and entrusted her with the command of a corps of troops. At the head of her soldiers, preceded by a banner with a picture of the Blessed Virgin, Joan succeeded in forcing the enemy to lift the siege of Orleans and in defeating them. The courage she showed in battle, trusting in Mary's help, is truly admirable.

In 1430, however, Joan fell into the hands of her enemies, who condemned her to the stake as a heretic. The heroine protested that she had never done anything but obey God's commands. Nevertheless, the sentence, though unjust, was executed, and she was burned alive in 1431 at Rouen, while invoking the Holy Names of Jesus and Mary.

Joan of Arc was beatified on April 18, 1909, by Pius X, and was canonized by Benedict XV on May 16, 1920.

Mother of grace and of life, of mercy and forgiveness, turn upon me your motherly countenance and raise me up to a state of perfect friendship with God.

CHAPTER XIII

THE WEDDING AT CANA

Left a widow by the death of St. Joseph, Mary changed her way of life very little. She tended to her home and went out only for errands of charity or religious duties.

It must not be believed, however, that Mary was negligent regarding her social duties such as visiting relatives and friends. Thus, as the Gospel narrates, she attended the marriage feast at Cana. "And on the third day a marriage took place at Cana of Galilee, and the Mother of Jesus was there" (John 2: 1).

It is a great joy for oriental women to participate in wedding preparations. Sisters, cousins and friends of the bride and groom assume the responsibility for the preparation of choice foods. They arrive at the home where the wedding is to take place on the eve of the feast, or even a few days before, and stay until the end, which is usually for about a week. The Evangelist has us suppose that Mary was already there with that family when her Son Jesus was invited. And Jesus went there with His disciples.

On that feast Mary proved the goodness of her heart toward the newlyweds, by inducing her Son to work a delicate miracle so as not to spoil the sweet joy of the day.

At a certain point, Mary noticed that there was no more wine. With a few words she pointed out to Jesus the young couple's preoccupation, and tactfully, as only she knew how to do it, begged Him to help them: "And the wine having run short, the Mother of Jesus said to Him, 'They have no wine' " (John 2: 3). Such a statement was obviously made to demand a miracle, and it reveals Mary's great confidence in her Jesus. She had always believed in her Son's divine power, and for thirty years she had experienced the goodness of His heart and His readiness to grant her least desire. She was, thus, certain of obtaining the miracle. Jesus, however, answered Mary in a way that emphasized the independence of His own action: "What wouldst thou have Me do, woman? My hour has not yet come" (John 2: 4).

Mary understood that He was postponing the miracle for a later time, but certain of being heeded, she told the servants: "Do whatever He tells you." And Jesus, indeed, gave them orders to fill the jars with water. There were six large stone jars prepared in accordance with the Jewish manner of purification, each holding two or three measures.

The servants filled the jars to the brim. Then Jesus said to them, "Draw out now, and take to the chief steward" (John 2: 8).

As soon as the latter had tasted the wine, not knowing where it had come from, he chided the groom for having saved the best wine for the last, contrary to custom: "Every man at first sets forth the good wine, and when they have drunk freely, then that which is poorer. But thou hast kept the good wine until now" (John 2: 10).

Thus in Cana of Galilee, Jesus worked the first of His miracles, and manifested His glory, and His disciples believed in Him.

This episode teaches us a valuable lesson. Jesus willed to perform His first miracle at Mary's urging in order to teach us with what trust we should have recourse to this Mother of goodness to obtain the graces we need.

Mary is good; she thinks of us, sees and provides for our needs. Mary knows our wants. Assumed into Heaven in soul and body, and admitted to the Beatific Vision, Mary sees in God all our thoughts, feelings, aspirations, difficulties, dangers, temptations and resolutions.

We are not excused by this fact from praying to her or enumerating the graces we need. Mary knows what is best for us, so let us tell her of our needs and trust in her. Let us abandon ourselves completely to her maternal heart.

Wedding at Cana

"And the wine having run short,
the Mother of Jesus said to Him, 'They have no wine.'"

(John 2: 3.)

1. Mary is powerful in her intercession.—The power of Saints to obtain graces is proportionate to their merit. Now, just as no one surpasses Mary in merits, likewise, no one has as much power of intercession. What God can do by commanding, you, O Virgin, can do by praying.

2. Mary's prayer is omnipotent because she has a mother's authority over her Son Jesus.—Therefore, let us go to Mary without fearing to ask too much, as long as we seek graces that are useful for eternal life, and we pray with the proper dispositions.

3. Mary wants to provide for us.—She is our Mother and a mother seeks the well-being of her children.

Mary wants us to be saints, similar to her, that we may reign with her in Heaven.

A Thought from St. Bernard: Perhaps the Lord's reply may seem quite hard and severe, but He knew to whom He was speaking; and Mary knew Whom it was Who was speaking. And that you may know how she received His reply and how she trusted in the goodness of her Son, she said to the servants, "Do whatever He tells you."

Fra Bartholomew's Painting

It was the year 1247. The Founders of the Servants of Mary in Florence entrusted to Fra Bartholomew, a distinguished and devout artist, the task of painting in their chapel a fresco depicting Mary in the act of receiving from the Archangel the annunciation of the Incarnation. The artist began the work at once. Soon, the fresco neared completion; only the faces of the Blessed Virgin and the Angel remained to be painted. The artist, however, felt incapable of giving expression to the great concept of the Annunciation. He attempted again and again in vain, until one day he fell asleep in utter discouragement. A few moments passed. Fra Bartholomew awoke, and beheld to his great astonishment, the faces of the Blessed Virgin and the Angel beautifully painted and with heavenly expression. Beside himself with joy he cried out, "A miracle!" The Religious and the people came running, and stood in speechless admiration before those heavenly figures painted miraculously.

And this is the miraculous painting of the Annunciation in Florence, before which even in our day the faithful gather in devout prayer.

Our most loving Mother, Treasurer of graces and Refuge of us poor sinners, we fly to your motherly affection with lively faith, certain that you will hear our prayers

CHAPTER XIV

MARY AND THE PUBLIC LIFE OF JESUS

When about thirty years of age, Jesus came out of His voluntary seclusion, and began to preach His heavenly doctrine. Before beginning His apostolic life, however, He went to His Mother to obtain her consent, or at least to inform her of His decision. Mary had foreseen this moment because she was well acquainted with Sacred Scripture and the prophecies. For some time the banks of the Jordan had been resounding with the voice of John the Baptist preaching penance, giving baptism as a sign of it, and assuring the people that the kingdom of Heaven was at hand. The time was ripe, and Jesus presented Himself to be baptized. As soon as John saw Jesus, he exclaimed, "Behold the Lamb of God, Who takes away the sins of the world!" (John 1: 29).

Afterwards Jesus retired into the desert for forty days, where, with fasting and prayer, He prepared Himself for His lofty mission. The name of Jesus, His miracles and His divine words soon became famous throughout Palestine. He made His home at Capharnaum, and many authors maintain that Mary did likewise.

1. **What did Mary do during the apostolate of Jesus?**—Three things: she prayed, she listened to His word, she followed Him and continued to serve Him.

a) **Mary prayed.** This is a most important mission, for prayer can do everything. Prayer is the base and the foundation of the apostolate, and without it we can do nothing. Fully aware of this, Mary prayed that her Son's apostolate might be full and fruitful.

b) **Mary listened to the word of Jesus.** Let us note Mary's unique position: on the one hand, she was superior to Jesus because she was His Mother; but on the other hand, she was inferior to Him because Jesus was the Son of God, sent by the Father! Mary became the humble and docile disciple of Jesus. She listened intently to all His words, and profoundly meditated them in her heart: "She kept all these things carefully in her heart" (Luke 2: 51).

c) **Mary served Jesus humbly.** When St. John Bosco began his mission, he took his mother with him, so that she might assist in the care and education of his boys. Jesus and His Apostles, too, were served by Mary, by the august Mother of the Word Incarnate.

Oh, the humility of Mary! "Behold the handmaid of the Lord" (Luke 1: 38).

2. **The Gospel records two instances in which Jesus spoke of His Mother.**—Jesus was going about

Palestine preaching the good tidings, curing the sick and freeing the possessed. From every side, He was assailed with so many supplications and petitions that He was often obliged to stop in the open country without being able to enter the towns. People followed Him about and welcomed Him as a great prophet and wonder-worker.

One day when Jesus was in the house of Simon Peter, intent on teaching the people, a messenger told Him, "Your Mother and brethren are outside seeking You." Jesus no longer had either mother or relatives; His family consisted of those souls who had come to Him to learn the glad tidings of the kingdom of God. And, resting His gaze upon His listeners, Jesus answered, "Behold My mother and My brethren! For whoever does the will of My Father in Heaven, he is My brother and sister and mother" (Matt. 12: 49-50).

With this reply, Jesus did not intend to belittle His Mother's greatness. He simply wanted to give the world a splendid lesson. He wished to teach us that above love of our family and relatives stands the love of God, and that the true greatness of a soul consists in doing God's will: "Not everyone who says to Me, 'Lord, Lord,' shall enter the kingdom of Heaven; but he who does the will of My Father in Heaven shall enter the kingdom of Heaven" (Matt. 7: 21).

How great is the dignity of a soul that does the will of God! Without a doubt, according to nature,

Mary's greatest dignity lies in being the Mother of Jesus, the God-Man. According to Faith, however, he is greater who does God's will. Mary was proclaimed Mother of Jesus in a twofold manner: physically and spiritually.

St. Luke narrates another episode in these words: "Now it came to pass as He was saying these things, that a certain woman from the crown lifted up her voice and said to Him, 'Blessed is the womb that bore Thee, and the breasts that nursed Thee.' But He said, 'Rather blessed are they who hear the word of God and keep it' " (Luke 11: 27: 28).

Again Jesus meant: Mary is blessed and is called thus not only because she is My Mother, but because she listened to the word of God and put it into practice. Blessed is he who listens to God's word and puts it into practice! "Blessed are they who hunger and thirst for justice, for they shall be satisfied" (Matt. 5: 6).

"Not by bread alone does man live, but by every word that comes forth from the mouth of God" (Matt. 4: 4).

Mary was the first guardian of Jesus and His first listener. This fact teaches us to love the apostolate and to love the word of God.

The apostle earns a twofold merit for having taught and acted well. Let us sanctify ourselves and do good to our neighbor.

A Thought from St. Bernard: The Blessed Virgin accompanied Our Savior in every phase of His life, and she, more than anyone else, took to heart all His words and deeds. She alone understood the Savior's remarkable words, the stupendous marvels of His preaching, His strong and tender words, His divine severity with the corrupt, proud world, with sin and with the prince of hell. She alone was the constant witness of all these deeds. She saw them in their proper aspect. She studied their meaning attentively, understood them well and engraved them deeply upon her memory. She impressed upon the minds of the apostles and disciples all that she had heard and seen. She faithfully communicated and implanted deep within their hearts all that she knew of the Word.

St. Bernard

St. Bernard was born in 1091 in Fontaines. He was the third of seven children and was consecrated to the Virgin Mary. When he was nineteen years of age, his mother died, and this saintly young man then turned trustingly to his heavenly Mother and told her, "You will be my mother." Mary indeed proved that she was his mother by protecting him from every danger, especially spiritual dangers.

Having overcome the world, he abandoned it, and together with thirty other companions won by his enthusiastic words, he retired into the solitude of the Cistercian monastery. Here, in the silence of the cloister, Bernard's love for Mary increased greatly. He thought of her continually and sought to imitate her in her virtues. His every act, word and thought was directed to Mary. Such a great lover and affectionate, constant devotee of the Mother of

God could not help but win her protection and benevo-
lence. From his boyhood to his death our Saint received
continual and very special favors from the Blessed Virgin.
During his stay at Chatillon, for example, he fell asleep
while waiting in church on Christmas night. He then saw
the mystery of the birth of Jesus exactly as it took place in
the grotto of Bethlehem, and the Blessed Virgin, handing
him the Holy Child said, "Take, Bernard, my Son, the Redeemer of the world."

On another occasion, in the year 1146, when he entered a church and greeted the Blessed Virgin three times,
she replied three times: "Hail, Bernard." Likewise, when
he hailed a statue of Mary with the words: "Hail, Mary,"
she deigned to answer him: "Hail, Bernard."

Consumed by hard work, fastings, watches, penance
and his most austere way of life, Bernard bid farewell to
his monks and dear ones on August 20, 1153, and became
recollected in himself. A mysterious light flooded his cell,
and Bernard sat up, stretched out his arms and smilingly
said, "I am coming." The Blessed Virgin, whom he had
loved so deeply, had come to take her beloved Bernard
into the kingdom of glory.

**Save me, O Mary, for you are my hope; save me from the
pains of hell, but especially from sin, which alone has power
to make me lose my soul.**

CHAPTER XV

THE SORROWFUL MARY

The public life of Jesus was drawing to a close, and the time was approaching in which Mary would have to make the greatest of sacrifices: the offering of Jesus as a victim for our salvation.

Jesus was hated by the leaders of the Jewish people, and Mary's heart suffered. She lived under the dread shadow of a sacrilegious crime, the victim of which was to be her own Son.

Her fears and anxieties seemed to vanish as if by magic with a new wonder, which was over in a short time: the triumphal entry of Jesus into Jerusalem. As He advanced, seated upon a donkey, the crowd spread their cloaks on the road before Him and, praising Him for His miracles, cried out: "Hosanna to the Son of David! Blessed is He Who comes in the name of the Lord! Hosanna in the highest!" (Matt. 21: 9).

This episode inflamed the wrath of the Pharisees to a greater pitch, and they sought every means of condemning Jesus to death. Mary knew of their poorly concealed hate and she felt in her heart the stab of the sword predicted by Simeon.

Meanwhile Judas, an apostle loved and taught by Jesus, had made an agreement with the Sanhedrin to betray his Master into the hands of His enemies.

The Divine Redeemer knew all this. The hour of His enemies had come, the hour of the powers of darkness, and so He bade Mary His last farewell.

How describe the Blessed Virgin's sorrow at that last embrace? "May the Lord's will be done," she must have said, thereby consenting to Jesus' laying down His life for the salvation of souls. Did she follow Him to the Last Supper? Was she there when He instituted the Most Holy Eucharist and gave His last sermon to His Apostles? Did she witness His agony in the Garden of Gethsemane? Did she see the kiss of Judas? The Gospel is silent on these points. And the many opinions vary, but we may surmise that if Mary was not actually present, she knew everything and kept herself informed of everything.

After the news of the horrible tortures inflicted upon her Son and the death sentence pronounced by the Roman governor, Mary resolved to walk beside the Divine Victim. During the public life of Jesus there are moments when we would wish to see Mary beside Him glorying in His triumphs, but we do not find her. Instead, she is beside the suffering Jesus.

Tradition narrates that Jesus, weighed down by His heavy Cross, had no sooner set out on the sorrowful Way of the Cross when Mary joined Him from a street which opened onto it. In her dreadful agony of soul, the Mother lifted her eyes to Him, and His eyes met hers.

Whoever is fortunate enough to make the Way of the Cross in Jerusalem will find the site of this encounter at the fourth station. A church has been built there dedicated to St. Mary of the Agony.

We know from the Gospel that when Jesus was apprehended, all His Apostles fled. But John, who followed Jesus and went into the house of Anna, probably knew of His condemnation.

He hastened then to Mary, placed himself at her side, and did not leave her alone during the terrible hours that followed.

Mary was probably prevented by the crowds of soldiers from following Jesus except at a distance. Perhaps she was able to be close to Him only when He hung from the Cross. St. John does not say when Mary reached her Son's side. He speaks of the crucifixion, the inscription placed upon the Cross, the division of Christ's garments and the casting of lots for His tunic. Then he writes, "Now there were standing by the cross of Jesus His Mother and His Mother's sister, Mary of Cleophas, and Mary Magdalene" (John 19: 25). Mary was not alone beneath the Cross; near her was a group of the holy women.

The Sorrowful Mother

"O all ye that pass by the way,

attend, and see if there be any sorrow like to my sorrow."

(Lam. 1: 12.)

The figure of Mary on Calvary stands out unique, grandiose, awesome. Mary ranked second to Jesus by virtue of the sublime mission she was fulfilling at that moment and the sorrows that were lacerating her soul.

Mary had ascended Calvary to put the seal on her mission as Co-redemptrix. There the Woman concurred in crushing the head of the infernal serpent. Near the tree of the Cross, Mary repaired what Eve had foolishly ruined one day beneath the seductive foliage of a very different tree. On Calvary Mary was proclaimed the universal Mother of all men, and losing her only Son, she acquired us all as adopted children.

"When Jesus therefore saw His Mother and the disciple standing by, whom He loved, He said to His Mother, 'Woman, behold, thy son.' Then He said to the disciple, 'Behold, thy Mother.' And from that hour the disciple took her into his home" (John 19: 26-27).

Mary at the foot of the Cross is the most moving picture of the whole Gosepl story. No one can contemplate her without feeling his heart pervaded by a deep, ineffable sentiment of compassion.

The Church Fathers and ecclesiastical writers have found great difficulty in expressing the full bitterness into which the Blessed Virgin's heart was immersed. St. Bernard terms her more than a martyr. Eadmer expresses the same concept in the following terms: "Your heart was truly pierced, O Mary, by the sword of suffering more intense than the bodily sufferings of all the martyrs. In fact, the most cruel tortures inflicted upon the martyrs' bodies were nothing in comparison to your passion, which in its immensity, lacerated every part of your soul and the most intimate affections of your all-loving heart."

Blessed Amedo wrote that Mary suffered more than any man of the most robust constitution could ever suffer. She suffered more than human nature can naturally suffer.

The Church compares the immensity of Mary's sorrow to the vastness of the sea and places these words on her lips: "O all ye that pass by the way, attend, and see if there be any sorrow like to my sorrow" (Lam. 1: 12).

To the mind of the Church, the sorrows of Mary surpass every limit of comparison: Mary is the **Queen of Martyrs.** Mary was the Queen of Martyrs, because she was the Co-redemptrix. In union with Jesus, she willed to make reparation for our sins.

How many times we ourselves have pierced Mary's heart with the sharp sword of offense to God! Let us resolve to avoid every sin and, as much as possible, to make reparation for the offenses given to the Hearts of Jesus and Mary.

A Thought from St. Albert the Great: Just as we are obliged to Jesus for the passion He suffered for love of us, we are also obliged to Mary for the martyrdom which, in the death of her Son, she willingly suffered for our salvation.

Armand Godoy

Born on the island of Cuba of Spanish immigrant parents, Armand Godoy wrote volumes in French which won him great renown.

He had made a rapid climb to fame when, weary of the affairs and the life of the world, he remembered that he had a soul—a poet's soul, in fact. Both the religious and artistic problem were happily resolved by him simultaneously; he humbly returned to God and joyously sang of his restored faith, thus imitating Copée, Huysmans, James and numberless other converts.

We particularly recall his "Ite Missa Est," a splendid poetic interpretation of the Holy Mass; also his "of the Canticle of Canticles at the Way of the Cross" and "The Litany of the Blessed Virgin."

Considering only this last book, "The Litany of the Blessed Virgin," we note that Godoy had the wonderful idea of explaining in poetry the titles we give to the Mother of God in the Litany of Loreto.

The literary value of this poem is varied: it cannot be assumed that his inspiration is always lyrical to the same degree, but throughout there is a sincerity, a humility, a tenderness and an ardent enthusiasm for the theme that rank Godoy high, indeed, among our religious poets.

"The Madonna," wrote Umberto Monti, in reference to Godoy, "is not only the Seat of Wisdom, but also Mother of good poetry, and our poets, if they draw near to her with reverence and devotion, will yet draw from David's harp new melodies to resound universally. The Madonna herself said that one day *all peoples would call her blessed.* We must not forget that there is room for all humanity in this blessedness of Mary, and who, if not a poet, should intone in the name of the Christian peoples a hymn of love and gratitude and praise to Our Lady?"

O sorrowful Virgin, all the trials, contradictions and infirmities which it shall please our Lord to send me I gladly offer to you in memory of your sorrows, so that every thought of my mind and every beat of my heart may be an act of compassion and love for you.

CHAPTER XVI

MARY AND THE RESURRECTION OF JESUS

After the bloody drama of the Cross, Mary withdrew in expectation of her Son's glorious resurrection. Whereas the small group of friends who had remained faithful to Christ doubted their Master's promise to rise from the dead, Mary preserved unaltered her tranquillity of soul, for she was certain of the triumph.

Those who approached her felt their hope confirmed, their faith renewed. The holy women, no doubt, drew near to Mary in those days. Among them there was a complete exchange of confidences, and Mary certainly inspired them to greater faith in the words of the Master which promised His triumph over death.

In speaking of the apparitions of the risen Jesus, the Gospel first mentions the apparition to Mary Magdalen. It is common belief, however, that the honor and consolation of Christ's first apparition upon His return to life was granted to Mary. She was the first to behold the Savior's glory, just as she had been the first to share His sorrows.

Christ's love for His Mother and particularly His manner towards her when He hung from the

Cross convince us that when He arose from the dead, He appeared first to Mary, before all others.

Cardinal Capecelatro wrote: "When Jesus arose from the dead, Mary was the first to reap the benefits of the great mystery. She was the first to embrace her Divine Son and she was the first to delight in beholding the new and heavenly youthfulness gracing that Body which she, most blessed among women, had given Him. She saw and felt her own body glorified in the glorified Body of her most holy Son. She kissed the wounds which were to be the happiness of Heaven and she rejoiced to the fullest in Him Who constituted her Paradise— Jesus, conqueror of sin and death, the restorer of mankind in God. Out of gratitude, love and His duty as a Son, Jesus came to fill His Mother with His glorified self. Reverently adoring and embracing her Son, Mary found her delight in that most blissful visit and her heart was set on fire with a new and most strong love. From that moment there began for Mary, already holier than the angels, a new life of perfection. Whoever would wish to describe it fully would have to have the mind and heart of Mary. And even she herself would not be able to do so fully, for human words would never be capable of expressing that which transcends everything human.

"The dignity of the Mother of God has a certain infinity, and from the moment when she embraced the risen Jesus, her life was gradually consumed by two most noble loves, which together possess the strength of maternity, and which have this maternity's perfection, sweetness, incentives. From that moment, she became ever and ever more desirous of being united with her Son and with her glorified children. And in this desire, as in a living flame, she slowly consumed herself until the day of her glorification."

Why is it that the Evangelists are silent about such an important event? Perhaps because Mary, ever faithful to her way of humility and reserve, kept even this favor buried in her heart so as to make of it a new subject for her silent meditations.

It must also be held that during the forty days He spent on earth after His resurrection, Jesus conversed with His Mother many times, and that she was present at the moving scene of His ascension into Heaven.

From the Acts of the Apostles, we know for certain that Mary was present in the Cenacle at the descent of the Holy Spirit on Pentecost. For ten days, about one hundred twenty persons had been assembled there, according to St. Luke's narration: "Then they returned to Jerusalem from the mount called Olivet, which is near Jerusalem, a Sabbath day's journey. And when they had entered the city, they mounted to the upper room where were staying Peter and John, James and Andrew, Philip and

Thomas, Bartholomew and Matthew, James the son of Alpheus, and Simon the zealot and Jude the brother of James" (Acts 1: 12-13). The author of the Acts expressly notes that Mary was among the apostles: "All these with one mind continued steadfastly in prayer with the women and Mary, the Mother of Jesus, and with His brethren" (Acts 1:14).

It was, therefore, a prayer meeting, a holy retreat, in which Mary surpassed everyone in fervor of prayer and depth of recollection. And the Holy Spirit infused in her a grace as superior to that received by the others as her dispositions were superior to theirs.

Let us reflect: Mary was the first to share in the glory of Jesus, because she had been the most closely united with Him in sorrow.

St. Paul's expression is alway true: "We suffer with Him that we may also be glorified with Him" (Rom. 8: 17).

If we know how to suffer with Jesus as Mary did, we shall share eternal glory with her.

A Thought from St. Cyprian: What can enrich us more with merit in this life and glory in the next than suffering patiently?

Leo XIII

Leo XIII was born at Carpineto of the Pecci family, noted for both nobility and faith. At his Baptism he was given the name Joachim. His parents were faithful to the

devout practice of reciting the Rosary and it was this prayer
that inspired in Joachim a tender love for the Queen of
Heaven and strengthened him against the temptations and
seductions of adolescence.

He was entrusted to the Jesuit Fathers, from whom
he learned to love the angelic St. Louis and the Blessed
Virgin. He combined ardent piety with assiduous study to
such a degree that at the age of twenty-two he received his
doctorate in theology from the Academy of Noble Ecclesi-
astics and shortly afterwards, his doctorate in canon law.

When consecrated a priest, he ardently desired to be
a missionary among the pagans, but God, Who wanted
him to be His Vicar, set him on a different path. He became the Apostolic Delegate to Benevento, to Perugia, then
Papal Nuncio to Belgium and finally he was elected Archbishop of Perugia. Death in the meantime snatched Pope
Pius IX from the Christian people. When the Conclave
assembled, all eyes turned to Cardinal Pecci, who was
elected Supreme Pontiff and took the name Leo XIII. In
the darkness of the times, Leo XIII appeared like a new
dawn, and if he diffused much light in the universe through
his great genius and indefatigable work, it cannot be denied that everything in him was the fruit of his devotion
and love for the Blessed Virgin. He wrote eleven encyclicals
on the Rosary and enriched this prayer with indulgences.
Mary blessed her devoted son with singular graces, crown-
ing them all with a saintly death.

**To you, O Mary, we give our bodies, our hearts, and our
souls; to you we give our homes, our families, our country. We
desire that all that is in us and around us may share in the
benefits of your motherly affections and care.**

CHAPTER XVII

MARY AND THE APOSTLES

Mary was made the Mother of God to be the apostle, that is, to give Jesus to the world. We have received all from Mary in Jesus Christ.

The title, "Queen of Apostles," is the most glorious after the title of "Mother of God." By her divine motherhood, Mary became Queen of Heaven and earth, of Angels and of men, and among the latter, particularly of the Apostles: "The queen stood on Thy right hand, (O King of Heaven), in gilded clothing; surrounded with variety" (Ps. 44: 10).

We read in the Acts of the Apostles that after Jesus ascended into Heaven, the Apostles descended the Mount of Olives and gathered in the Cenacle with Mary and the other holy women in expectation of the Holy Spirit.

The Divine Paraclete, promised by Jesus, descended upon them, bringing light, grace and comfort.

1. **Mary was an example to the Apostles.—** When she was immersed in a sea of sorrow and love at the foot of the Cross on Calvary, Mary's faith did not fail. Stronger than Abraham, she offered her only Son to the Father, with the intention of offering everything for the redemption of the

world. When Jesus was laid in the sepulchre, the Apostles doubted His resurrection; Mary alone kept the light of faith burning and strengthened the Apostles in this virtue. It may very well be said that the faith of the primitive Church was entirely gathered in Mary!

Furthermore, Mary was an example of fervor, zeal, strength and temperance. When the first persecutions broke out, Mary consoled, comforted, and sustained the Apostles and the faithful with her example, her words, and especially with her prayers.

2. **Mary was the counsellor and light of the Apostles.**—After the ascension of Jesus, Mary did not abandon the Apostles but was often with them. She loved them as an affectionate mother and instructed them as a competent teacher. What a sublime picture it is to contemplate Mary in the midst of the Apostles! With what ardor and dedication did she speak to them of Jesus! It was Mary who told the Apostles of those little incidents, now sorrowful and now joyful, concerning Christ's infancy and adolescence. And from whom did St. Luke learn the facts he relates in the first pages of his Gospel if not from Mary? Rightly then did St. Anselm exclaim: "Notwithstanding the descent of the Holy Spirit, many great mysteries were made known to the Apostles by Mary."

The Church is the continuation of the life of Jesus Christ; it is His Mystical Body. And Divine

Descent of the Holy Ghost

The Divine Paraclete, promised by Jesus,
descended upon them; bringing light, grace and comfort.

A. Gaber

Providence acted according to a plan of goodness, entrusting to Mary's care the infant Church as It had first entrusted her with the care of the Infant Jesus. Cornelius A Lapide wrote that Jesus left the Virgin on earth that she might be Mother of the Apostles and of the first faithful, that she might lift up the fallen, comfort the afflicted, strengthen the weak, counsel the doubtful, direct, instruct and inspire everyone.

As long as the first faithful and Apostles had their Mother Mary with them, they felt more certain of the assistance and protection of her Son Jesus.

3. **Mary was the comfort of the Apostles.**—How many times the Apostles must have had recourse to Mary and recommended themselves to her prayers! They had been present at the wedding at Cana and had witnessed Mary's power over the heart of Jesus. Therefore, when they felt weak and discouraged, they had recourse to her. Before leaving for distant lands to preach the Gospel, they recommended themselves to Mary and asked her blessing. And Mary blessed them, comforted them, and encouraged them.

Mary assembled and encouraged the Apostles when Christ's capture had scattered them and put them to flight. She sustained and comforted Peter who was disheartened over his denial of Jesus, and she inspired him to have confidence and to be certain of forgiveness. She brought serenity and

trust during the early persecutions, when the fury
of Christ's enemies rose against the Church, and
sought to annihilate it in its infancy, imprisoning
the Apostles. Mary sustained and taught those who
were persecuted to bear and overcome adversities.
How beautiful it is to imagine the Apostles prostrate
at Mary's feet receiving her maternal blessing! If
they were so strong in the face of obstacles, it is
certainly because they found comfort and help
in Mary.

What Mary Most Holy did for the first Apostles
she does also for us. Therefore, let us consider Mary
as the Queen of every apostolate. Let us take refuge in her and await everything through her intercession. Let us carry out our apostolate under
her maternal gaze.

Mary is an example to the Apostles of all times.
She gave Jesus to the world; let us, too, give Him
with every means at our disposal! May our apostolate always be performed in a supernatural
manner—never for human reasons.

Mary is also our wise counsellor. Let us have
recourse to her in every doubt, uncertainty and
temptation. **Look at the star, invoke Mary.**

Devotion to Mary, Queen of Apostles, is a
guarantee for the success of the apostolate.

Let us conduct ourselves in regard to Mary,
Queen of the Apostles, as the Apostles themselves
did. They loved her, they venerated her, they

prayed to her, and they had recourse to her in every need.

Protected by Mary, we shall labor for the coming of Jesus Christ's kingdom with greater efficacy, and the greater devotion we have to her, the more souls we shall save. **To Jesus through Mary.**

A Thought from St. Anthony: Jesus wanted His Mother Mary to remain in the world for a certain period of time after His ascension, that she might be the Mistress and Guide of the Apostles.

The Seven Words of the Blessed Virgin

With the exception of the Magnificat, Mary's words were few and brief but most meaningful. The Gospel records seven phrases uttered by Mary.

The first was one of virginal reserve: "How shall this happen, since I do not know man?" (Luke 1: 34).

The second was one of faithful obedience: "Behold the handmaid of the Lord; be it done to me according to thy word" (Luke 1: 38).

The third was one of reverent modesty: she "saluted Elizabeth" (Luke 1: 40).

The fourth was one of grateful joy: "My soul magnifies the Lord" (Luke 1: 46).

The fifth was one of authoritative gentleness: "Son, why hast Thou done so to us?" (Luke 2: 48).

The sixth was one of tender charity: "They have no wine" (John 2: 3).

The seventh was one of firm faith: "Do whatever He tells you" (John 2: 5).

Most holy Virgin of the Cenacle, obtain for us, we humbly pray, the gifts of the Holy Spirit, that we may live in charity and persevere in prayer, under your guidance and protection.

CHAPTER XVIII

MARY'S LAST DAYS ON EARTH

Many writers affirm that after the descent of the Holy Spirit, Mary lived for a time in Jerusalem and then in Ephesus, the city of Mary.

The dying Jesus had entrusted His Mother to His beloved disciple, John, who testified that he had at once taken her into his home (John 19: 27).

During this period of waiting for Heaven, Mary presented to Jesus, now glorious in Heaven, the needs of the infant Church and its Apostles. She prayed for the neophytes, she prayed for the conversion of idolaters and sinners. Her heart grew ever more inflamed with the desire to be reunited to her Son.

After the ascension of Jesus into Heaven, the following words can very well be attributed to Mary: "As the hart panteth after the fountains of water; so my soul panteth after Thee, O God" (Ps. 41: 2). It was her ardent desire for Heaven which led her to exclaim, "My soul hath thirsted after the strong living God; when shall I come and appear before the face of God?" (Ps. 41: 3).

The desire for Heaven is fundamental, for faith in our rewarding God is one of the principal and essential dogmas. When a person is convinced of this truth and has faith, he establishes his life upon God alone and is indifferent to all else. To him, the important thing is to win Heaven. Hope in this great reward must gladden us: "I rejoiced at the things that were said to me: we shall go into the house of the Lord" (Ps. 121: 1). It should make us exclaim with St. Francis: "The good that awaits me is so great that every pain is a delight to me."

Mary's life on earth drew to a close. Her eyes were fixed on Heaven; her heart beat with affection for God; her face shone and a smile was ever on her lips. All at once her heart gave a start, and Mary flew to Heaven, to the embrace of her Beloved.

1. **Mary was consoled in her last days on earth by the great number of her merits.**—Life passes rapidly, time flies and we continually add merits or demerits to the book of life. Every thought, sentiment and action is a merit or demerit according to whether it is good or bad, and whether or not it was accomplished with the right intention.

What was Mary's condition at the end of her earthly life? She had merits only, no sin—neither original, nor mortal, nor venial. Nor was there any voluntary imperfection in her actions, but all was perfect and meritorious. Mary, moreover, did not begin from nothing as we do, but rather from the point where the merits of the greatest Saints reached, since she was superior to all the Angels and Saints from her Immaculate Conception: "The fountains thereof are in the holy mountains" (Ps. 86: 1); Mary was "full of grace" (Luke 1: 28).

This grace continued to increase in Mary until the last moment of her earthly life. How, then, is it possible for the human mind to calculate the treasure of grace accumulated by her?

Struck with admiration at the sight of the great merits adorning Mary at her entrance into Heaven, the Angels asked, "Who is she that cometh up from the desert, flowing with delights, leaning upon her beloved?" (Cant. 8: 5).

Are all our thoughts, sentiments and actions holy? Great vigilance is necessary. Let us try to sanctify all our days living with faith, hope and charity.

2. **At the thought of her continuous progress in virtue, Mary experienced great consolation during her last days on earth.**—He who draws nigh to God and converses with Him is holy. Sanctity increases according to the progress man makes in his union with God. No one was ever more closely united to God than Mary.

If sanctity consists in fleeing from sin and practicing virtue, where can one find a person who avoided offending God and faithfully practiced virtue more than Mary? If sanctity consists also in presenting "your bodies as a sacrifice, living, holy, pleasing to God" (Rom. 12: 1), who conformed to this conduct more than Mary? "She was holy, holier than all Saints: a treasure of sanctity" (St. Andrew of Crete).

The fire of God's love ever grew in Mary until it became so violent that she flew to Heaven in an ecstasy of love—worthy crown of such a holy life!

If we wish to close our earthly pilgrimage as Mary did, let us try to imitate her in her daily progress.

Let us resolve to aspire to sanctity at all costs and to make some progress in virtue every day.

An apostolate done for Jesus will greatly console us at death; all the fatigue we endured to fulfill the apostolate will be of great consolation to us.

May the Queen of Apostles obtain a holy death for all; it is the most important grace that we can desire.

A Thought from St. Jerome: Mary not only aids her servants at death, but also comes to meet them when they pass from this life to the next, so as to encourage and accompany them to the divine tribunal.

St. Pius V

On January 7, 1504, Pius V was born in Bosco of the noble and ancient Ghisleri family.

Since his parents were poor, the child did not find material comforts in his home, but rather affectionate care, good example, sound moral training and especially a great love for the Blessed Virgin. He soon felt the desire to consecrate himself to God, but poverty did not permit him to enter the seminary. Mary, whom he loved tenderly, came to his aid.

One day he met some Dominican Fathers who having noticed his keen, precocious genius, piety and candor of soul, promised to accept him in their order. With great joy, Michael ran home and obtained permission to enter the Dominican monastery at Voghera. He progressed rapidly in both piety and his studies.

When ordained a priest, he dedicated himself entirely to the education of the young seminarians, always inculcating in their hearts a tender love for the Queen of Heaven. Renown of his sanctity soon became widespread and he was made inquisitor of the faith for Lombardy: he carried out this office with extreme prudence and ability. In 1556 he was elected Bishop of Nepi and Sutri. Soon after, he was elected Cardinal.

At the death of Pius IV, the Sacred College of Cardinals elected Cardinal Ghisleri Supreme Pontiff. Pius V was truly great; he was esteemed by all, including heretics, for whose conversion he worked tirelessly until his death. But that which really immortalized this Pope's name was the famous victory of the Christians over the Turks at Lepanto—a victory obtained by Pius V through his great confidence in the Blessed Virgin. In the beautiful month dedicated to Mary Most Holy, he went to his reward, laden with merits and bearing his baptismal innocence.

Mary most holy, Mother of goodness and mercy, obtain for me the grace to call upon you more frequently, so that I may breathe forth my spirit with your sweet name on my lips and the Name of your dear Son.

CHAPTER XIX

MARY ASSUMED INTO HEAVEN

There is a vast difference between Saints and followers of the world. Although the latter have some small successes, some rare satisfactions amid the trials of life, everything ends for them with death. Saints, instead, bear the inevitable sorrows of exile with resignation, **"for the yoke of Jesus is easy, and His burden light"** (Matt. 11: 30), but in the end, they will receive the eternal reward which the Lord prepares for those who love Him. Saints will have a more tranquil death and a happy eternity, whereas worldlings, after a life often full of misery, will have an unhappy eternity, too. People who detach themselves from the goods of the earth while they live will not have to do so at the point of death. At that hour, instead of leaving behind they will gather the fruit of their virtue: "And everyone who has left house, or brothers, or sisters, or father, or mother, or wife, or children, or lands, for My Name's sake, shall receive a hundredfold, and shall possess life everlasting" (Matt. 19: 29).

If this is the lot of the Saints, what was the lot of Mary, the most excellent of creatures? Having entered the world through a series of graces and

privileges, Mary ended her earthly pilgrimage with
a new prodigy: God, Who had created her immaculate, willed that she be assumed into Heaven in
soul and body. She who was conceived without sin
was not to see the corruption of the grave. The
Co-redemptrix was to reign in Heaven with the Redeemer; she was to take her place near the throne
of God to intercede for all mankind: "Come from
Libanus, my spouse, come from Libanus, come:
thou shalt be crowned" (Cant. 4: 8).

1. **Mary is in Heaven in body also.**—Mary was
exempt from original sin and her body was justly
glorified immediately after her earthly life. She
enjoys all the prerogatives of risen and glorious
bodies: impassibility, clarity, agility and subtileness.

"Mary," says St. Bernard, "is presented to us
clothed with the sun. She, in fact, who is immersed
in God's inaccessible light, has penetrated the infinite abyss of divine wisdom much more deeply than
man can imagine."

Mary is the noble star of Jacob whose rays
brighten the entire world, shine in the heavens, en-
circle the earth, warm souls, quicken virtue and
reduce vice to ashes.

Mary's body is now glorious, like the Body of
Jesus. It can fly with the speed of thought from
place to place; it can pass through locked doors;
it no longer is subject to the weaknesses of human

nature because it is spiritualized. Why was Mary's body so privileged? Because in life it was most docile to her soul, submissive in everything to reason. Mary progressed from good to better; in her there was no rebellion of body against spirit. It was just, therefore, that her body, which had shared her soul's merits, should also share its glory immediately.

Every merit has a corresponding glory in Heaven.

2. **Mary was exalted above the choirs of Angels and the Saints.**—Thus sings the Church in the liturgy of the Assumption. Behold the triumph of her who professed herself to be the humble Handmaid of the Lord. There is no earthly comparison we can make to get an idea of the welcome given to Mary in Heaven. For her, all the choirs of Angels were moved to action, and even God Himself displayed His magnificence to receive her. At her entrance into Heaven innumerable bands of Angels accompanied her and called to those who came to meet them, "Hasten, O Princes of Heaven, arise, open the portals, for the Queen of glory must enter in."

When she entered Heaven, Mary was welcomed by the Blessed Trinity, before Whom she prostrated herself in humble adoration, while the Angels and Saints came to pay homage to her as their Queen. To her was given a throne of glory superior to that of the Angels themselves as the Liturgy attests.

Mary was thus exalted because she had so deeply humiliated herself. Her throne was placed close to Christ's, for in life she was always close to Him.

Let us learn from Mary to live in humility: only he who knows how to humble himself will be exalted by God.

3. **Mary was crowned Mediatrix and Dispenser of graces.**—Seated on her radiant throne, the Blessed Virgin was proclaimed by the Blessed Trinity Queen of Heaven and earth, Mediatrix and Dispenser of every grace. Mary's throne is the throne of mercy, and her mission in Heaven is continually to ask that the merits of Jesus be applied to us, that our sins be pardoned and that all necessary graces for eternal life be granted to us. In Heaven Mary is the good and powerful Queen who showers endless blessings upon earth.

St. Bernard says: "Take away the sun, which warms, illumines and makes everything fruitful, and what would remain on earth but dense fog and a deathly chill to sadden all nature? Likewise, if the shower of graces poured upon us by God's Mother were to cease, what would remain for men but anguish, sorrow and death?"

A Thought from St. Modestus: Hail, O most holy Mother of God! God Jesus, King of glory, Who chose you to be His spiritual palace here on earth and Who willed at the same time to give us the kingdom of Heaven through you, wanted you with Him in this kingdom—intact in body and surpassingly glorious. He willed this for the greater glory of His Father and the Holy Spirit.

Mary, the Inspiration for Art

There has never been a great artist, sculptor, poet or composer worthy of the name who has not been devoted to Mary, to her who, in the words of the poet, "ennobled human nature."

The seer of Patmos, St. John, beheld the triumph of the Woman clothed with the sun and adorned with the stars. He beheld and was enraptured with joy as he heard celestial spirits singing the hymn of victory.

It was only right that the Angels should sing to Mary, to her before whom all creation bows. Mary is the garden of delights that God found as pure as Heaven's Angels. She is the source from which springs the stream of water that bathes the earth. She is a paradise adorned by the most beautiful flowers. For this reason poetry, painting and music have dedicated their greatest masterpieces to Mary; this is why artists and poets will never cease to admire her and to reproduce this masterpiece of beauty.

Poetry has a most genial sister: music, and our men of genius did not fail to use it in the service of the Virgin.

Poets and musicians are followed by painters and sculptors. Raphael, nourished from early childhood with devotion to the Madonna, portrayed her with rare grace and charm. Fra Angelico knelt while painting his Madonnas. Guericino, enamoured of Mary, began to paint her when he was only ten years old.

In view of such splendor and great affection for Mary, are we to be the only silent ones? Yet how shall we sing the praises of our heavenly Mother? Let us love her, pray to her and have complete trust in her. "What is sweeter," writes St. Basil, "what is better, more salutary or more delightful than thinking and speaking of the Blessed Virgin?"

Beauty and glory demand love. Mary is a star, a flower that enchants and attracts. Man is fascinated and runs to her. He hastens to her when life is sad and filled with afflictions; he runs to her in joys and experiences all the tenderness of a Mother, all the strength of a Queen and all the joy of the Blessed One. Let us praise Mary! After God she is our greatest glory and our deepest joy. Kneeling before her revered picture, let us say to her each day: "O star of the sea, August Mother of God, shatter the bonds that shackle sinners, shine your light in the eyes of the blind, free us all from evil. Grant that we may be meek and pure, and show us the surest way to Jesus. Virgin Mary, Mother of Jesus, make us Saints."

O my heavenly Queen, you have no other desire but to see your Divine Son loved by men. Obtain for me the grace of an ardent love of Jesus Christ, so that my heart will seek God alone.

PART III

MARY IN HER LIFE OF GLORY

CHAPTER I

MARY IN HEAVEN

Mary Most Holy had a triple life: she lived in the mind of God and on the lips of the Prophets; she led a natural life, which is believed to have lasted between sixty-five and seventy-five years; and she lives in Heaven and in the hearts of her devotees.

What is Heaven? It is the reward for souls who work; the recompense, the crown of justice for souls who have fought for the Lord.

1. **In Heaven souls see, possess and enjoy God.**— Mary's life in Heaven is like that of the blessed souls about her, with the exception that she sees, possesses and enjoys God in a much more perfect manner.

In Heaven the soul sees God. Our eyes see when there is light, for this is the medium of vision without which we see nothing, even if our eyes are open. In Heaven God Himself will be the light of our soul, which will acquire the power of seeing spiritual things: "The just will shine forth like the sun in the Kingdom of their Father" (Matt. 13: 43); "we shall see Him just as He is" (1 John 3: 2). "The blessed," says St. Augustine, "see God without any

interruption, they know Him without fear of being
subjected to any illusions, they love Him without
danger of offending Him, they praise Him without
ever growing tired."

What is the medium for seeing God in Heaven?
It is no longer natural light, but it is God Himself.
"In Thy light we see light" (Ps. 35: 10). "The Lamb
is the lamp thereof. And the nations shall walk by
the light thereof; and the Kings of the earth shall
bring their glory and honor unto it" (Apoc. 21:
23-24). St. Paul says, "We see now through a mirror
in an obscure manner, but then face to face. Now
I know in part, but then I shall know even as I
have been known" (1 Cor. 13: 12).

There is a difference, however, between one
soul and another: the Beatific Vision is in proportion
to merit. The Blessed Virgin had the greatest merit
imaginable, for she was full of grace.

She penetrated God's mysteries more than any
Angel or Saint. O what light is revealed to Mary
Most Holy!

Merit in general determines the strength of
our eye to see God, but the merit that enables us to
see the most is the merit of faith. He who has
believed and tried to know God better on earth will
see Him better. The Lord will manifest Himself
more to souls who possessed a more lively faith:
"as thou hast believed, so be it done to thee"
(Matt. 8: 13).

How is the spirit of faith acquired? By exercising it and by asking God for it in prayer. Whoever listens to God's word and meditates upon it progresses in faith, as does he who makes frequent acts of faith, recites the Creed devoutly, believes the Church and entrusts himself to Her as a child to his mother.

No one certainly had greater faith than Mary Most Holy: "blessed is she who has believed" (Luke 1: 45). No one in Heaven, therefore, has entered so deeply into the knowledge of God as Mary Most Holy.

2. **Heaven is the possession of God.**—On earth there are many good things; they are all means that the Lord grants us to serve Him more faithfully and to acquire merits for Heaven. But the true and only supreme good is God. In Him is gathered every good—every perfection—in an infinite manner. "Great is the Lord," says the regal prophet, "and greatly to be praised: and of His greatness there is no end" (Ps. 144: 3).

"For who shall search out His glorious acts?" (Ecclus. 18: 3). Who can ever describe the wealth of a soul that possesses God? In Heaven Christ's prayer to the Father finds its complete fulfillment: "That all may be one, even as Thou, Father, in Me and I in Thee; that they also may be one in Us" (John 17: 21). God is all in all His chosen souls so as to manifest all His power in them that there may be light, health, virtue, abundance, glory, honor, peace and every good thing.

"Who will succeed in understanding," exclaims St. Bernard, "the multitude and immensity of joys contained in the words: God is all in all? He is the fullness of light for the intelligence, the perfect possession of every good for the will, eternity for the memory. O Truth! O Love! O eternity! O Blessed Trinity Who render us blessed, my miserable trinity (intelligence, will, memory) pants after You, because it is unfortunately far from You. Hope in God and every error will vanish from your intelligence; your will will relinquish every resistance; every terror will depart from your memory, and in its place will come a marvelous light, a perfect serenity, an eternal security and joy."

In Heaven, therefore, the souls possess God, but not in the same way, even though all are completely happy. "Star differs from star in glory" (1 Cor. 15: 41). That which constitutes the varying capacity for possessing God are the merits of each one. Those who are wealthier in merits are also more capable of possessing God. Mary, the richest in merits, possesses and enjoys God in a more perfect degree.

Which is the merit which renders us more capable of possessing God? It is conformity to the Divine Will.

Let us consider God as our final goal: let us become detached from the world and let us try to love the Lord ever more deeply. If we love God above all else from now on, we certainly shall go to enjoy Him in Heaven, for "charity never fails" (1 Cor. 13: 8).

3. **Heaven is joy in God.**—"Enter into the joy of thy master" (Matt. 25: 23). God will give Himself to each one of the elect that they may enjoy Him.

The soul is invited to share in the very happiness of God Who, as He gave us our being, will likewise give us His glory. The blessed in Heaven contemplate God's majesty, they enjoy His delights, they admire Him, they praise Him, and they love Him.

Mary's joy is the fullest. More than all the blessed, she enjoys the peace, the glory and the happiness of being with God.

St. Augustine very well describes the great joy of the elect. In Heaven there is no trace of evil and suffering, and every good thing abounds. There, hymns are sung to the Lord Who is all in all: "Blessed are they that dwell in Thy house, O Lord: they shall praise Thee for ever and ever" (Ps. 83: 5). The elect devote themselves to praising God.

In Heaven only is there true glory. In Heaven there is true honor, which is not denied to anyone who deserves it and is given only to those who are worthy of it. In Heaven there is the culmination of happiness, supreme glory, infinite joy, and an abundance of every good. "And how could You help but give Your elect a torrent of pleasures from which to drink, O Lord," exclaims St. Bernard, "when You poured the oil of Your mercy even upon Your crucifiers?"

"Let us therefore hasten to enter into that Rest," says St. Paul (Hebrews 4: 11).

Who can ever describe the happiness of the blessed? "What are your delights, O lovers of God?" asks St. Augustine. "You take delight in the abundance of peace. Your gold is peace, your silver is peace, your possession is peace, your life is peace, your God is Peace—all that you desire will be peace! There, your God will be everything for you; you will eat of Him so as not to be hungry, you will drink of Him so as not to be thirsty, you will be enlightened by Him so as not to be blind, you will be supported by Him so as not to fall. He will possess you and you will possess Him entirely."

If the joy of privileged souls favored by singular graces is so great on earth, what can be said of the blessed in Heaven? Up there is found the greatest good: the soul will be completely immersed in God. An infant who dies immediately after Baptism will have greater joy and greater happiness than people who are considered happy on earth. Even in this respect, Mary will surpass all. . . .

The more devout a soul is on earth, the more it will share in the joy of God. Mary's piety was the most perfect. What fervent prayers of adoration and supplication, what holy aspirations she raised to God! They were as sighs of a dove departing from her heart, rising to God. What acts of love Mary made in the stable as she adored her God and her Son! And in the humble house at Nazareth? Rightly does the Liturgy affirm that in admiration, Angels hastened to that little house to learn from its celestial inhabitants how to pray to God and adore Him.

Mary was the most sublime example of a prayerful soul, and for this reason she now enjoys God in Heaven in the most perfect manner.

We must acquire a strong spirit of piety. "Godliness is profitable in all respects" (1 Tim. 4: 8). Does your piety resemble Mary's?

We must dedicate our best time to prayer. Are we always faithful to our practices of piety? Do we always fulfill them with fervor?

Let us beg Mary for her spirit of piety.

A Thought from St. Anselm: Mary's love for us neither ceased nor diminished after her assumption into Heaven. It rather increased there, for now she sees human miseries all the more. How unfortunate we would be if Mary did not lovingly pray for us from Heaven.

St. Teresa of Jesus

In 1517, when Luther initiated his false reform, Teresa Ahumanda was born in Avila through a wondrous disposition of Divine Providence. She was the Saint who was to bring great good to God's Church, and who was to play an important role in arresting the progress of the heresy.

By their example and teachings, her parents trained a large family in the practice of Christian virtue. At a very early age, Teresa displayed a keen interest in reading books which, according to the trends of the time, were written in a romantic fashion.

The story of martyrs so deeply impressed her noble heart and that of one of her brothers that they decided to leave home secretly to go to the land of infidels—where they, too, would become martyrs. They had already started their journey when their uncle met them just as they arrived at the city walls and brought them back home. An unfortunate disaster, however, befell that family. Teresa became very friendly with a worldly relative, who soon led her along the ways of vanity. When her father grew aware of this, he enrolled her as a student in an Augustinian monastery in Avila. The constant examples of piety and virtue given by the Religious soon restored Teresa's desire for eternal goods.

Becoming seriously ill, Teresa had to return to her family, but the beauty of religious life as contrasted with the world's vanity had made a deep impression upon her. Mary Immaculate nurtured in the child Teresa the desire to consecrate herself to God and to enter Carmel. She soon received the religious habit and took her vows. God ever enriched Teresa with great and extraordinary graces, and she progressed rapidly in the way of perfection.

Enlightened by Heaven, she decided to reform the Carmelite Order. With the help of St. Peter d'Alcantara and the Dominicans who directed her, she founded the first Discalced Carmelite convent in 1562, in Avila. She dedicated it to St. Joseph. In spite of grave opposition and persecution, Teresa undertook the foundation of other monasteries, and she wrote mystical treatises.

She died on October 4, 1582, after a long ecstasy of fourteen hours.

In 1591, the process was initiated for her beatification. In 1622, only forty years after her death, she was canonized by Gregory XV.

Pray, O Mary, pray and never cease to pray until you shall see me safe in paradise, where I shall be sure of possessing and loving my God together with you, my dearest Mother, forever and ever.

CHAPTER II

DEVOTION TO MARY

The Blessed Virgin leads the entire heavenly court in singing praise to the Blessed Trinity. As St. Francis de Sales expresses it: "Her voice rises above all others, rendering more praise to God than does any other creature."

For this reason, the celestial King invites her in a special way to sing: "shew me thy face, let thy voice sound in My ears: for thy voice is sweet, and thy face comely" (Cant. 2: 14).

About herself, Mary gathers choirs of Angels and Saints and intones the Magnificat, the most sublime hymn of thanksgiving.

However, Mary does not live in Heaven only; she continues to live in the Church and in the heart of every faithful, who venerates her with a special and affectionate devotion.

Veneration for the Blessed Virgin began when she was still on earth. The Archangel Gabriel appeared to her and greeted her with words of the highest praise: "Hail, full of grace, the Lord is with thee. Blessed art thou among women" (Luke 1: 28). St. Elizabeth honored her with inspired praise: "Blessed is the fruit of thy womb" (Luke 1: 42). And what can be said of the great reverence that St. Joseph, Mary's most chaste spouse, had for her? But more than anyone, her divine Son, Jesus, esteemed and venerated her. He loved, obeyed and respected her; He gave Himself completely to her and willed to depend on her for everything. All the Apostles rendered homage to Mary, especially St. John, the privileged one who took her into his home after the death of Jesus. The Magi, the shepherds, and all who were so fortunate as to make her acquaintance venerated Mary.

In the meetings of the early Christians, Mary always held a place of honor, as the Acts of the Apostles reveal. The account of the disciples assembled in the Cenacle after Jesus' ascension into Heaven records Mary's presence and she alone, of all the faithful, is mentioned by name.

Through the Gospel, devotion to Mary became widespread among Christians, and we have the first manifestations of Marian devotion.

After the Council of Ephesus, love and veneration for the Mother of God grew considerably by reason of the abundance of literature defending, explaining, illustrating the dogma of Mary's Motherhood. It was during the eleventh century, however, that devotion to Mary assumed an eminent position. St. Anselm, St. Bernard and other holy Doctors wrote much about Mary, propagating her devotion in a wonderful manner. Mary came to be honored, exalted and invoked because of her privileged relationship with the Son of God made man.

Marian devotion is scriptural, evangelical and ecclesiastical.

The Holy Bible presents to us a Woman foretold by Prophets and represented by types indicating aspects of the beauty which would be hers. This Woman is praised and sought after.

The Gospel also speaks of this exalted Virgin. The Archangel Gabriel inaugurates this with his most gracious and magnificent homage. Elizabeth adds her voice to the voice of the Angel, proclaiming Mary blessed. The shepherds and the Magi bow to her. Jesus Himself honors His Mother by living in obedient and devoted subjection to her.

Devotion to Mary, proclaimed Mother of all mankind by the dying Jesus, is deeply rooted in the Catholic Church. It was passed down from the Apostles to the first disciples; from the first disciples to the martyrs, to the virgins, and to the confessors. It has grown in century after century, in generation after generation, to become a vital, important part of Christian, Catholic cult.

Let us make every effort to guard this devotion as a precious treasure inherited from our fathers that we may be able to hand it down to posterity.

Who can describe the benefits of devotion to Mary? She not only listens to her devotees, she anticipates their petitions and grants them beyond all expectations.

Let us take Mary for our Mother, and let us have recourse to her every morning and evening and in life's difficult trials: Mary will comfort and save us.

Let us remember that we have a Mother in Heaven. "Behold your Mother!"

A Thought from St. Albert the Great: Mary anticipates souls that come to her so that they may find her before they seek her.

Contardo Ferrini

Contardo Ferrini was born of devout parents in 1859. He received a fine Christian upbringing to which he corresponded fully. After successfully completing his classical studies, he went to the University of Pavia where, because of his precocious mind, he acquired a high degree of learning in a brief span of time.

In this young man's room, an image of Mary, Seat of Wisdom, occupied a place of honor. To her, he had entrusted his future. At the age of twenty-two, he received his degree in law, and at twenty-four, with a rich and profound cultural background, he embarked upon his career as Professor of History of Roman Law. He spoke Latin, Greek, Hebrew, German, French, English, Syrian and Spanish fluently.

He soon began to publish important works, and he diligently responded to the vocation he received from God by breaking and distributing the bread of truth among the ignorant. He led a retiring, humble, charitable, and virtuous life, always practicing the evangelical counsels.

Contardo Ferrini wrote pages of great beauty on various feasts of Mary. Regarding the feast of the Annunciation he comments as follows on the words, *Behold the handmaid of the Lord; be it done unto me according to Thy word:* "Never before was such true and wondrous humility expressed; never before was any creature raised to such stupendous honors by God and who was at the same time so convinced of her nothingness. It has been well said that Mary pleased God because of her virginity but conceived Our Savior because of her great humility."

Regarding the feast of Mary's Visitation, Ferrini said: "Elizabeth greets her. . . . And Mary feels very lowly as she considers God's tenderness, for she realizes that He wills to choose little ones for great deeds and that His goodness is greatest toward the weak. Then she bursts into that hymn which we should intone with the Angels after Communion: 'My soul magnifies the Lord.' He is to be admired who can find cause for humility even from praise."

Contardo retained the obedience and simplicity of a child until his death. To these qualities he joined a great spirit of mortification, which he had learned from the example of Mary.

At the age of forty-three, already rich in merit, he went to the Heaven of his desires, close to the Virgin, whom he had so greatly loved.

O Mary Immaculate, the precious name of Mother of Good Hope, with which we honor you, fills our hearts to overflowing with the sweetest consolation and moves us to hope for every blessing from you.

CHAPTER III

MARY'S APPARITIONS

From time to time, down through the centuries, the Blessed Virgin has deigned to descend among her children in a visible manner. She always does so for two reasons: for the greater glory of God and the salvation of souls.

Mary's apparitions have been numerous. Some of them have been recognized by the Church; they are of such a nature and there is so much evidence in support of their validity that they cannot be rejected. Let us consider a few of these apparitions approved by the Church and included in the Holy Breviary, that we may better understand Mary's love for men.

1. **The Apparition to the Seven Founders.**—In 1233, the Blessed Virgin appeared to seven noblemen of Florence while they were absorbed in prayer. She advised them to give up their worldly goods and honors, retire from the world, and thus serve her with greater purity and fervor. They quickly responded to the invitation of their celestial Queen Mary and distributed their riches to the poor. Then,

dressed in humble clothes, they retired to Villa Camozia, where they led a life that was more angelic than human.

When they returned to Florence in 1234 to confer with the Bishop, crowds ran to meet them, and through a marvelous prodigy tiny infants praised them crying out, "Here are the Servants of Mary! Here are the Servants of Mary!" Among these children a five-month-old infant miraculously pointed these men out to his mother with the words, "Mother, here are the Servants of Mary! Give them alms!" He then fell silent and spoke no more until he reached the age when children normally begin to speak. This child became a Saint—St. Philip Benizi, who was admitted to the Servants of Mary at the age of twenty. Through his work the Order expanded greatly, especially in France and Germany.

After this singular prodigy, fame of the virtue of the seven Religious became so widespread that people the world over sought their advice and prayers.

On Good Friday evening, March 25, 1240, while they were meditating upon the Passion, Heaven opened to them, and they beheld the Blessed Virgin in a dark mantle accompanied by a legion of Angels carrying the instruments of the Passion. One of them held a palm, another held a black Habit, a third carried St. Augustine's rule, and a fourth carried a shield which bore the inscription,

"Servants of Mary," written on a blue background. As soon as the heavenly Queen approached them, she said: "I am the Mother of God, who chose you for my servants. Under this title, you will cultivate my Son's vineyard. Here are the Habits which you will wear in the future." And thus speaking, she gave a black Habit to each of them.

"The color of these Habits," continued Mary, "will suffice to keep ever present in your memory the bitter sorrow I felt at the Crucifixion and death of my only Son. Propagate devotion to my Son's Passion and my sorrows. Follow the rule of St. Augustine, and be my faithful servants by founding a new Order of Religious under the title: **Servants of Mary.** Let this palm which you see, be for you a reminder of the glory prepared for you in Heaven if you honor me on earth." With these words, Mary disappeared.

Blessed by Mary, this Order spread, and its apostolate bore marvelous fruits not only in Europe but also in the Missions. Pope Leo XIII canonized the Seven Holy Founders.

2. The Apparition to St. Jerome Aemiliani.—
St. Jerome was born of the noble Aemiliani family in Venice in 1480. As a young man, he was so successful in his career that by 1512 he was already purveyor of the Venetian Republic. However, when Venice was attacked by enemy soldiers, Jerome was

taken prisoner and received inhuman treatment in
a dungeon. Moved by his tears and supplications,
the Virgin deigned to appear to him and free him.

Having obtained his freedom, Jerome began a
new life. He decided to devote his attention to poor,
neglected orphans, and he was the first to found
orphanages, which are one of the great credits to
Christian charity.

Friends of his who were desirous of consecrat-
ing themselves to the service of God and neighbor
joined him. And thus was born the Congregation
of the Somaschi.

3. **The Apparition to St. Catherine Labouré.**—
Three apparitions were made to Catherine Labouré
which were recognized by the Church. The first occurred on July 18, 1820, at 11:30 P.M. Catherine
heard the delicate voice of a charming child calling
her—a child whom she considered to be her Guardian Angel. He invited her to go to the chapel and
there she saw the Blessed Virgin, who confided
several matters to her, predicted the horrors of the
revolution of 1870, and gave her some salutary advice. On November 27 of that same year the second
apparition occurred. "The Virgin was of medium
stature," St. Catherine later revealed. "She was
dressed in a loose fitting, high necked robe with
large sleeves. A white veil fell from her head to her
feet. She was standing on a globe about which a

large serpent was entwined. Her foot was set on his head to crush it. Her eyes were lifted to Heaven, and in her hands, which were raised to the level of her breast, she held a globe surmounted by a Cross. This she was offering to God with an expression of prayer.

"All at once the globe disappeared from her hands and her fingers suddenly became encircled with gems that sent off dazzling rays. She lowered her arms, showering torrents of splendor upon the globe on which she stood. The Virgin said that the globe represented the world and the rays symbolized her graces. Next, an oval frame formed about Our Lady and around it, written in gold, were the following words: **O Mary, conceived without sin, pray for us who have recourse to thee.** And a voice added: Have a medal coined upon this model; people who wear it around their necks will receive great graces."

Then the frame turned and on the other side the Saint saw the letter M surmounted by a Cross. Beneath the letter were two hearts; one encircled by a crown of thorns, the other pierced by a sword. A crown of twelve stars bordered the frame.

The third apparition occurred about a month later.

Catherine was elevated to the honors of the altars by Pius XI and devotion to the Miraculous Medal increased steadily.

4. **Mary's Apparition at Lourdes.**—From the time the Mother of God visited it in her apparitions, Lourdes has been a place of heavenly predilection, graces and miracles. On February 11, 1858, Bernadette Soubirous, a simple and innocent girl, went with two companions to gather wood near the shore of the River Gave.

When she reached the lonely grotto of Massabielle, she beheld, in a niche radiating the purest light, the figure of a marvelously beautiful lady, who appeared very kind and gracious. She was dressed in a robe as white as snow, caught with a blue sash. Her hands were folded and she held a white Rosary with a gold chain. She was rapt in prayer. As Bernadette gazed upon that celestial vision, she knew not its meaning. The radiant Lady then began to pass her fingers over the beads, indicating to Bernadette how dear the recitation of the Rosary was to her. After the recitation of the Rosary, the vision vanished.

The Blessed Virgin appeared seventeen more times, exhorting the girl to pray for sinners and to do penance. She commanded her to go to the priests with the request that a shrine be erected in that very location so that the faithful could go there.

One day, in answer to Bernadette's request to know her name, the sweet Lady lifted her eyes heavenward, folded her hands and said, "I am the Immaculate Conception." Within a short time the fame of the miracles at Lourdes became well known, and the Church recognized the authenticity of the apparitions.

5. **The Apparition at Fatima.**—On May 13, 1917, three children of Fatima, Portugal, were watching their sheep and reciting the Rosary, when suddenly lightning flashed. Fearfully they looked at the sky, but there was not a cloud. In fact, the sun was shining brightly. They decided to go home, but as they led their sheep forward, an even brighter flash of lightning paralyzed them with terror. A chill passed over them. Then, looking to the right, they beheld a most beautiful and radiant Lady, more brilliant than the sun, standing on a small holm-oak tree. She turned to them saying, "Fear not, I wish you no harm." The Lady wore a garment as white as snow, gathered at the neck by a golden cord; a white mantle embroidered in gold covered her whole person. From her joined hands fell a Rosary of pearl beads, at the end of which was a silver crucifix. Her countenance was luminous but sad. Lucy, the oldest of the three shepherd children, courageously asked her:

"What country are you from?"

"My country is Heaven."

"And what have you come to do?"

"I have come to ask you to come here on the thirteenth of every month for six consecutive months. In October I shall tell you who I am, what I have come to do, and what I want."

"You come from Heaven! And am I going to Heaven?" asked Lucy.

"Yes," answered the Lady.

"And Jacinta?"

"She, too."

"And Francis?"

The Virgin gazed upon the boy and said, "He, too, but first he will have to say many Rosaries."

With that she disappeared.

News of the apparition spread rapidly in Fatima, and subsequently throughout Portugal and the world.

At the last apparition, on October 13, 1917, the crowd gathered at the Cova da Iria was immense: 70,000 persons were there. It had been raining during the night and it was still raining at daybreak; but as a proof of their faith and devotion, the pilgrims patiently accepted their discomfort.

At midday there was a flash of light—the sign that Our Lady was coming. Lucy then asked the beautiful Lady: "Who are you, and what do you want me to do?"

The Vision answered: "I am the Lady of the Rosary! I ask that a shrine be erected here in my honor. I have come to plead with all the faithful to amend their lives, to beg pardon for their sins, and to resolve never to offend the Lord again. Continue to say the Rosary every day. I promise that, if men will change their sinful life, I will answer their prayers, and the war will end soon."

After lengthy and diligent examination, ecclesiastical authorities declared the apparitions worthy of faith and gave permission for devotion to Our Lady of Fatima.

Many more of Mary's apparitions could be cited, but we have chosen the above-mentioned because of their valuable teachings.

A Thought from St. Bernard: The Lord placed in the hands of Mary all the graces He wishes to give us, in order that we may know that whatever good we receive passes through her hands.

Raphael

On Good Friday, March 28, 1483, Raphael was born. He learned the fundamentals of painting from his father, John, a good artist. Later he studied with Perugino. Under the influence of this teacher he painted the "Coronation of the Virgin" for the Vatican Galleries, and "Mary's Espousals" for the Brera Gallery. It was in this manner that this devotee of God's Mother began to honor the one who was the supreme love of his heart.

Raphael established himself at Florence, where he felt the beneficial influence of the art of Leonardo da Vinci and Fra Bartholomew. About 1507, he painted his first great historic picture: the Deposition. Shortly after this work he was called to Rome by Pope Julius II to decorate the Vatican rooms. Here Raphael revealed his genius and attained to artistic perfection. His love for the all-beautiful Queen of Heaven continued to grow and he manifested it in the numerous and splendid Madonnas he painted.

Mary protected him throughout his life, but especially at the hour of his death, which occurred on Good Friday, April 6, 1520.

From thy throne of mercy, turn your pitying gaze upon us, O Mary, and upon our families, upon our country and upon the universal Church. O Mother, stay the arm of your unheeded Son's justice and win the hearts of sinners by your mercy.

CHAPTER IV

MARIAN SHRINES
THROUGHOUT THE WORLD

In the history of Christianity, Marian Shrines are monuments through which generations affirm that Mary is their august, celestial Queen. They are monuments of Mary's Queenship on earth. They are oases of peace, mercy and love. They are the Virgin's regal villas—thrones where she dispenses special graces and privileges from time to time.

Marian Shrines are numerous, and the faithful are accustomed to make pilgrimages there in Mary's honor, to implore her maternal protection. When a Christian is stricken with moral or physical infirmities which resist every cure, he seeks health and blessings in one of these places of devotion. There, only virtue and sanctity prevail, and divine grace abounds; there infirmities and weaknesses of soul and body are cured or at least mitigated.

Shrines are like convalescent homes of piety where souls acquire new life and new energies. There are Marian Shrines throughout the world, and their origin can almost always be attributed to some extraordinary grace or manifestation of the Blessed Virgin.

Shrine of Our Lady of Loreto

Most revered is the **Shrine at Loreto** which includes the Holy House of Nazareth, miraculously transported there by Angels on December 10, 1225, after a series of prodigies. A splendid basilica, which was restored and embellished several times in the course of centuries, was built around it. The Holy House is in the center of the basilica, under the cupola, and on the exterior it is adorned by the magnificent bas-relief by Sansovino. The miraculous statue of the Virgin, placed in the niche behind the altar, is covered by a most precious robe. Lamps of gold and silver continuously burn in the Holy House. Loreto became the earthly, royal palace of the celestial Queen: approximately fifty Popes, the most powerful Catholic sovereigns, many Saints and millions of faithful visited this Shrine in order to receive through Mary light, grace and comfort.

The Shrine of Our Lady of Pompeii

The Blessed Virgin's temple which is majestic in appearance and imposing in size is built in the form of a Latin cross. At the main altar reigns the portrait of Our Lady of the Rosary in the midst of a halo of light. From dawn to sunset there is a continuous stream of faithful in the sanctuary who gather there to receive the Sacraments, to recite the Rosary and to sing praises to the Blessed Virgin.

Only God knows all the graces that the Madonna of Pompeii has showered advantageously upon her devotees.

The Shrine of Our Lady of Lourdes

Of all the Shrines in the world where the heavenly Queen loves to shower her graces, there is none perhaps that better commemorates her compassion than the Shrine of Lourdes. The origin of this Shrine is connected with Mary's apparition to Bernadette Soubirous in 1858. Lourdes has become the goal of continuous pilgrimages. Numerous miracles take place there publicly—before great crowds in broad daylight, and they are investigated by a board of doctors.

Shrine of Our Lady of Victories in Paris

The origin of this Shrine is moving. The faithful of the parish of Our Lady of Victories did not go to church, nor did they care about their eternal salvation. Consequently, their Pastor was greatly concerned. One day, right after he had begun to celebrate Mass, at the words, "Judica me, Deus," the priest heard an interior voice saying: "You are nothing, your work is sterile, your ministry useless. . . . It would be better for you to give up. . . ." This was a distressing thought which he sought in vain to dismiss. Before the Canon of the Mass, he paused briefly and invoked the Lord's help as well as Mary's. Then he heard these words echoing clearly in his soul: "Consecrate your parish to the Immaculate Heart of Mary." After obtaining the Archbishop's approbation, the good Pastor inaugurated the Confraternity of the Immaculate Heart of Mary for the conversion of sinners, and soon after, the series of miracles began in Paris which became known throughout the world.

The Shrine of Our Lady of the Pillar in Saragossa

The origin of this Shrine is very ancient. Tradition connects it with St. James the Greater, the Apostle of Spain. When taking leave of Mary and imploring her blessing before departing for the missions, St. James heard her say to him, "Go, my son, fulfill the commands of the Divine Master. In a city in Spain where you will have a great number of believers, remember to build a church dedicated to my name in the place I shall show you." Having reached Spain, St. James went from city to city preaching the Gospel. At Saragossa he converted a great number of people and spent many hours with them in holy exercises of prayer.

One night he heard celestial melodies, and looking up, he saw the Blessed Virgin enveloped in a radiant light and accompanied by a choir of Angels. She stood before him on a pillar, called him by name and expressed the desire to see a church erected there. "The pillar," added Mary, "will always stand firm on this spot to testify that Christian faith will never depart from these shores. Let the altar of my Shrine rest upon the pillar and this place will become a throne of graces for souls who come to invoke me." St. James fulfilled Heaven's wishes by constructing a Shrine in Mary's honor. Our Lady of the Pillar has always been venerated by the Spaniards.

The Shrine of Our Lady of Guadalupe

The story of this splendid Shrine is truly beautiful.

At daybreak on December 9, 1531, a recently converted Indian peasant named Juan Diego was on his way to Tlatelolco to assist at Mass. When he reached the foot of Mount Tepeyac he heard sublime, joyous melodies that seemed to come from Heaven. In amazement he lifted his glance to the hill from which the celestial music seemed to be coming, and he beheld a pure white cloud over which there rose a glorious rainbow. While the good Juan Diego ecstatically watched the spectacle, he heard a voice call him by name. It urged him to hasten on.

As he hurriedly left the mount in obedience to the command, he saw a woman of divine beauty standing in the midst of the light. Her countenance was as resplendent as the sun, and rays of dazzling light departed from her robe.

"My son, whom I love tenderly," she said, "where are you going?"

"Beloved Lady, I am going to Tlatelolco to assist at Mass which is being celebrated in Mary's honor."

"I praise your devotion, my son, and your humility of heart pleases me. I want you to know that I am the Virgin Mother of God. It is my wish that a church be built in this place wherein I shall reveal that I am a loving Mother to you, and to all souls who will confidently invoke my name. Go to the Bishop, tell him that I sent you and narrate faithfully what you have seen and heard."

Fray Juan de Zumarraga, first Bishop of Mexico, did not believe the story at first, but after repeated apparitions and miracles, he believed and fulfilled everything the Virgin desired. The wonderful image miraculously depicted on poor Juan Diego's rough cloak was placed in the richly decorated Shrine and is still preserved there today. The colors of the picture look as fresh and bright as though it had just been painted.

The National Shrine of the Immaculate Conception in Washington, D. C.

In 1846, twenty-two Bishops representing the twenty-eight states then in the Union consecrated the country to Mary Immaculate. It was a gift of sequoias and Spanish moss, of waterfalls and can-

Our Lady of Guadalupe

From time to time the Blessed Virgin has deigned
to descend among her children in a visible manner.

yons, rolling hills and long plains; a gift of a young and great people—of millions and millions of hearts —of countless little people, free people, who would constantly renew the gift of themselves to Mary.

It was a wise plea to Mary for help. There is always need for a mother who can help and who cares so much to help.

To complete this plea the National Shrine of the Immaculate Conception at Washington, D.C., has been dedicated to honor the Blessed Virgin Mary as the Patroness of the United States. The Shrine project was begun in 1914, and the foundation stone was laid in 1920. When completed, the Shrine, situated on the campus of the Catholic University of America, will be one of the ten largest churches in the world.

The building has the form of a cross. It will have an external length of 459 feet, and an external width of 240 feet and an internal height, under the dome, of 159 feet. The facade will be dominated by a bell tower 316 feet in height, one of the greatest in the world. In addition to the main altar, the upper church will have side chapels and nearly 50 altars; it will have a seating capacity of 3,000 and a total capacity for 6,000 persons.

Peoples of every nationality and faith are proud of this magnificent national Shrine, and are certain that the Immaculate Conception, although enjoying the splendors of Heaven, does not forget the world, nor her children, whom the dying Jesus entrusted to her maternal care.

Along with other Marian Shrines scattered throughout the world, **La Salette Shrine** in Grenoble and the **Shrine of Fatima** in Portugal should be mentioned. Both of these had their origin following apparitions of Mary.

When it is possible to visit some shrine or church dedicated to Mary, let us do so willingly. If this is impossible, in spirit let us join the souls who gather at the feet of the Blessed Virgin and let us beg her to extend her graces to us.

A Thought from St. John Damascene: Mary's Shrines are cities of refuge where we find escape from temptations, and from the punishments we deserve for our sins.

A Pilgrimage

In order to demonstrate their genuine and resolute will to resist persecutors at any cost, the Mexican Catholic population celebrated the Feast of Christ the King with large pilgrimages to the venerated shrines in various cities during the year of the most bitter persecution. With great enthusiasm an exceptional pilgrimage was made to the Basilica of Our Lady of Guadalupe, Patroness of the entire Mexican nation. In fact, a multitude of more than 300,000 people, among whom were women of the highest level of society, filed barefoot past the Madonna's venerated image in a continuous stream from 5:30 A.M. to 7:00 P.M.

A member of the pilgrimage, eye-witness of these events, expressed in these few words the emotions of sadness and joy that filled every heart: "It cannot be said that the ceremony of national consecration to our divine King and to Our Lady of Guadalupe was solemn, for that which constitutes Catholic worship was lacking, that is, the Holy Sacrifice of the Mass. Jesus in His most august Sacrament was missing, nor was there at the altar a Priest, the minister and representative of Christ. It can be well said, however, that it was an unprecedented spectacle, for never before had so many thousands of Catholics been seen to kneel at the feet of our Mother and Queen of Guadalupe, renewing our full and total consecration to her divine Son, Jesus Christ, before her miraculous image. Once again we confirmed our unswerving fidelity to the Church and to its Supreme Head, the successor of Peter, to whom Our Lord addressed those words which are the foundation of our hope in these days of cruel presecutions: 'The gates of hell shall not prevail.'"

O Mary, remember what ineffable power your Divine Son has given you over His adorable Heart, and since you are our Mother, graciously receive our prayers and grant our request.

CHAPTER V

THAT MARY MAY LIVE IN ME

Devotion to Mary is the fragrance of our faith, the heavenly smile to the faithful, the note of joy in our hearts, the dearest throb of our Christian life.

1. **Reasons for devotion to Mary.**—The first reason for devotion is love, and therefore, for the same reasons we love Mary we also are devoted to her. These reasons can be reduced to seven:

a) **God's special love for her.** "God loves the Virgin alone more than all the other Saints together," writes Father Suarez. St. Bonaventure, St. Anselm, St. Augustine and others affirm the same thing. Our Lady is so greatly loved by God because she is the most beautiful creature, both in the natural and the supernatural order: "I came out of the mouth of the most High, the firstborn before all creatures" (Ecclus. 24: 5).

b) **Her dignity.** God can create a firmament that is richer with stars, a more immense ocean, a more fertile land, but He cannot create a greater Mother, for there cannot possibly be a mother greater than she who calls God Himself her Son.

From this great honor of divine Motherhood, as from an inexhaustible source, immense treasures flow to Mary.

c) **Mary's sanctity.** Willing His Mother to be the most loved and most honored of all creatures, God made her the most worthy of love and honor. Thus He enriched her with more graces than all the Angels and Saints together.

d) **The devotion that the Church has had to Mary through every century.**

e) **The benefits obtained through her intercession.**

f) **The love she bears us.**

g) **The sign of eternal predestination that this devotion brings with it.**

Whoever avoids Mary encounters death; whoever finds Mary finds life.

2. **Qualities of true devotion.**—It must be **interior, tender, holy, constant,** and **unselfish.**

Interior: that is, it must begin from our heart and must stem from our esteem for Mary and from our knowledge of her greatness.

Tender: that is, it must be full of confidence. The soul must have recourse to Mary as to a good and true mother in all its needs with great simplicity, trust and tenderness—in doubts, to be enlightened; in temptations, to be sustained; in weakness, to be strengthened; in falls, to be uplifted; in discouragement, to be encouraged; in scruples, to be freed from them; in crosses and adversities, to be consoled.

Holy: that is, it must lead the soul to avoid sin and imitate Mary's virtues, especially her profound humility, obedience, faith, constant prayer, purity, ardent charity, heroic patience and angelic sweetness.

Constant: that is, it must strengthen the soul in virtue and render it courageous in opposing the maxims of the world, the desires of the flesh, and the temptations of the devil.

Unselfish: that is, it must lead the soul to seek God alone rather than self.

A true devotee of Mary does not serve this august Queen because of self-interest but simply because Mary deserves to be served. He does not love her because he hopes to receive favors but bcause she is amiable. Thus a devotee loves and serves Mary faithfully in aridity as well as in times of sweetness and sensible consolations.

How dear to God and His Blessed Mother is such a devoted soul.

3. **Foundation of true devotion to Mary.**—Devotion to Mary has its foundations in God, in Jesus Christ, in the Church, in Mary herself, and in the Liturgy.

In God: Mary was in the thought and will of God from all eternity: "I was set up from eternity"

(Prov. 8: 23). In the terrestrial paradise God promised our fallen first parents a Woman who would crush the devil's head: that Woman was Mary. God inspired the prophets to speak of her, of her privileges and her gifts. He raised up magnanimous women to prefigure her. He preserved her from original sin from the first instant of her conception. He filled her with graces. He associated her with the work of Redemption and crowned her life with her glorious Assumption into Heaven.

In Jesus Christ: for Mary lived, worked, and prayed with Him, and with Him she shared the joys and sorrows of family life. As the Redeemer, He willed her to be Co-redemptrix.

In the Church: which was founded beneath Mary's gaze, and which, with her help, began to spread. The Church invoked Jesus and Mary with the same hope and always united Mary's amiable feasts to the majestic feasts of Jesus.

In Mary herself: Because of her mission and virtues Mary deserves our respect, our confidence, our love and our devotion. The greatness of her Divine Son Jesus reflects such a resplendent light of nobility and sublimity on her that one cannot help venerating and loving her.

Lastly, devotion to Mary also has a **liturgical** basis. The Liturgy, even the most ancient, favors Marian devotion. In the Liturgy attributed to St. James we read: "Let us commemorate the Holy

Immaculate, most glorious and blessed Mary, our Lady, Mother of our God and ever Virgin."

The Liturgy of St. John Chrysostom says: "Let us commemorate the most holy, most pure and most blessed of all creatures, Mary, our glorious Lady, Mother of God, ever Virgin." In the most ancient Liturgy of the Ethiopians we find these words: "Rejoice, O Virgin, always; at all times offer our prayers to God so that our sins may be forgiven; intercede at the throne of your Son, so that He may have compassion on our souls." Finally the Blessed Virgin is commemorated in the Latin liturgy so that she may obtain protection and help from God for all the faithful.

Thus Mary has every right to our devotion, love and veneration; let us respond generously.

In the sublime canticle of the Magnificat, Mary says that the time will come when all nations "shall call me blessed" (Luke 1: 48). With these words she announces and predicts her greatness and this prophecy is admirably fulfilled throughout the ages. The venerated name of the great Mother of God echoes gloriously everywhere, in civilized as well as in uncivilized countries!

May your devotion, O Mary, grow, increase and expand as long as there are men on earth and Angels in Heaven! As long as God will be God! But it most assuredly will be like this and I shall ever rejoice, O my Mother, for you are worthy of every praise. Obtain for me the grace that I may honor, love, beseech and imitate you on earth so that I may be able to enjoy your company in Heaven forever.

Long live Mary, her name, devotion and love!

Let us resolve to pray to the Blessed Virgin especially with the recitation of the Rosary. Mary will reign in our heart and if Mary is with us, what can we fear? With Mary's love in our heart we shall attain eternal salvation.

A Thought from St. Bernard: Let us try to venerate this divine Mother Mary with all the affections of our heart, for it is God's will that we receive every grace through Mary's hands.

"Here Lives a Freethinker"

On May 17, 1926, a priest wrote from Namur—I was curate of.... In this city lived a man who placed a sign over his door which read: "Here lives a freethinker."

This man became seriously ill and was in danger of death. In spite of the sign over the freethinker's door, being the curate, having a responsibility for this soul, I knocked on the door. Upon seeing me, the dying man cried out violently:

"My rifle, my rifle, give me my rifle!" In fact, a rifle was hanging over his bed.

"It matters little, my friend," I answered. "You want your rifle and I shall give it to you"....

"Ah, you are not afraid," he added with surprise. "This astounds me."

"No, my friend, I am not afraid."

He did not shoot, in fact, we soon began to chat a bit.

After a few days the freethinker agreed to accept, as his nurse, his own sister, who was a Religious. One of the first tasks of that holy soul was to remove the famous sign from his door. Not long after I was able to administer the Sacraments to the sick man. After this, surprised at my success, I said to him:

"Well, you are fortunate. All your life you have been a rascal. You did all the harm you could possibly do in this life; nevertheless, you are going to Heaven!"

"I hope so," he answered.

Then I asked him to what he attributed such a great grace. He answered frankly:

"To the Blessed Virgin. On the day of my first Communion I promised to recite my three Hail Mary's daily, and I never failed. This was my only religious practice."

O Mary, dearly beloved Mother, how close to God you are and how utterly filled with Him! Obtain for me the grace of loving my Jesus; obtain for me the grace of loving you.

ST. BONAVENTURE'S
MARIAN TE DEUM

We praise you, O Mother of God, we proclaim you Virgin and Mother!

The entire world venerates you as Spouse of the Eternal Father!

And to you all Angels, Archangels, Cherubims and Seraphims sing unceasingly:

Holy, Holy, Holy is the Mother of God, Mary ever Virgin!

Heaven and earth are filled with the majesty of your Son!

You are honored as Queen by the whole heavenly court!

You are invoked and praised as Mother of God by the entire world and by the holy Church.

You are the gate of Heaven, the ladder to the kingdom of Heaven and blessed glory!

You are Spouse and Mother of the eternal King, the temple and sanctuary of the Holy Spirit; the altar of the Blessed Trinity.

You are the Mediatrix between Jesus Christ and men, the Advocate of the poor!

You are, after Jesus, our only hope, Mistress of the world, Queen of Heaven!

We bow to you and salute you each day, O Mother of love!

Sweet and good Mary, in you we place all our hope, defend us for all eternity!

Amen.

Daughters of St. Paul

IN MASSACHUSETTS
   50 St. Paul's Ave. Jamaica Plain, Boston, MA 02130;
      617-522-8911; 617-522-0875;
   172 Tremont Street, Boston, MA 02111; **617-426-5464;**
      617-426-4230
IN NEW YORK
   78 Fort Place, Staten Island, NY 10301; **212-447-5071**
   59 East 43rd Street, New York, NY 10017; **212-986-7580**

   625 East 187th Street, Bronx, NY 10458; **212-584-0440**
   525 Main Street, Buffalo, NY 14203; **716-847-6044**
IN NEW JERSEY
   Hudson Mall — Route 440 and Communipaw Ave.,
      Jersey City, NJ 07304; **201-433-7740**
IN CONNECTICUT
   202 Fairfield Ave., Bridgeport, CT 06604; **203-335-9913**
IN OHIO
   2105 Ontario St. (at Prospect Ave.), Cleveland, OH 44115; **216-621-9427**
   25 E. Eighth Street, Cincinnati, OH 45202; **513-721-4838**
IN PENNSYLVANIA
   1719 Chestnut Street, Philadelphia, PA 19103; **215-568-2638**
IN FLORIDA
   2700 Biscayne Blvd., Miami, FL 33137; **305-573-1618**
IN LOUISIANA
   4403 Veterans Memorial Blvd., Metairie, LA 70002; **504-887-7631;**
      504-887-0113
   1800 South Acadian Thruway, P.O. Box 2028, Baton Rouge, LA 70821
      504-343-4057; 504-343-3814
IN MISSOURI
   1001 Pine Street (at North 10th), St. Louis, MO 63101; **314-621-0346;**
      314-231-1034
IN ILLINOIS
   172 North Michigan Ave., Chicago, IL 60601; **312-346-4228;**
      312-346-3240
IN TEXAS
   114 Main Plaza, San Antonio, TX 78205; **512-224-8101**
IN CALIFORNIA
   1570 Fifth Avenue, San Diego, CA 92101; **714-232-1442**
   46 Geary Street, San Francisco, CA 94108; **415-781-5180**
IN HAWAII
   1143 Bishop Street, Honolulu, HI 96813; **808-521-2731**
IN ALASKA
   750 West 5th Avenue, Anchorage AK 99501; **907-272-8183**
IN CANADA
   3022 Dufferin Street, Toronto 395, Ontario, Canada
IN ENGLAND
   128, Notting Hill Gate, London W11 3QG, England
   133 Corporation Street, Birmingham B4 6PH, England
   5A-7 Royal Exchange Square, Glasgow G1 3AH, England
   82 Bold Street, Liverpool L1 4HR, England
IN AUSTRALIA
   58 Abbotsford Rd., Homebush, N.S.W., Sydney 2140, Australia